True Essence

Finding your authentic self without compromise

Judy Newbery

The Creative Female
PUBLISHING

True Essence: Finding Your Authentic Self Without Compromise
Author: Judy Newbery

Published by The Creative Female Publishing
Blackburn, Victoria
Australia

judynewbery.com

Contact publisher for bulk orders and permission requests.

First edition © 2023 Judy Newbery
This edition © 2025 Judy Newbery

Cover concept by Tamara Tyson for **3 ferns** » 3ferns.com
Cover & page design & formatting by Leesa Ellis of **3 ferns** » 3ferns.com

All rights reserved. No part of this publication may be reproduced, distributed, or transmitted in any form or by any means, including photocopying, recording, or other electronic or mechanical methods, without the prior written permission of the publisher, except in the case of brief quotations embodied in critical reviews and certain other noncommercial uses permitted by copyright law.

Please note that all information in this book is the opinion of the author obtained through her research, knowledge and the included references. The author does not give out any medical advice or suggest any techniques for physical, emotional or spiritual support. The information in this book is not meant to replace medical advice and a medical opinion should always be obtained for any health condition. The author and publisher except no responsibility, if you use any of the information in this book.

Printed in the United States of America.

ISBN (Hardcover): 978-0-6455612-3-4
ISBN (Paperback): 978-0-6455612-4-1
ISBN (e-Book): 978-0-6455612-5-8

CONTENTS

Introduction i

CHAPTER ONE	Roles	1
CHAPTER TWO	Growing Up	9
CHAPTER THREE	My Father	19
CHAPTER FOUR	My Mother	25
CHAPTER FIVE	Childhood Roles	31
CHAPTER SIX	Sex and Religion	35
CHAPTER SEVEN	Friendships	41
CHAPTER EIGHT	Role Models	47
CHAPTER NINE	Family	51
CHAPTER TEN	Mothering	61
CHAPTER ELEVEN	The Night The Stars Went Out	69
CHAPTER TWELVE	The Unknown	75
CHAPTER THIRTEEN	Letting Go	83
CHAPTER FOURTEEN	Losing Myself	89
CHAPTER FIFTEEN	Who Am I?	93
CHAPTER SIXTEEN	Caring	101
CHAPTER SEVENTEEN	No Is An Actual Word	109
CHAPTER EIGHTEEN	What's On The Other Side?	121
CHAPTER NINETEEN	Emotions	127
CHAPTER TWENTY	Rock The Boat	133
CHAPTER TWENTY-ONE	Playing The Victim	139
CHAPTER TWENTY-TWO	Worth	147
CHAPTER TWENTY-THREE	Forgiveness	155
CHAPTER TWENTY-FOUR	Yes	159
CHAPTER TWENTY-FIVE	Open Your Heart	165
CHAPTER TWENTY-SIX	True Essence	171
CHAPTER TWENTY-SEVEN	Be Yourself	177
CHAPTER TWENTY-EIGHT	Where To From Here?	187
CHAPTER TWENTY-NINE	A Time To Fly	195

Acknowledgements 204
References 205

This book is for my mother Katherine, my sisters Cathy and Sue who have always loved, encouraged, and inspired me, and for Neil and James whose love and support make everything possible.

Introduction

Women throughout history have shaped the roles of women today and enabled them to have the freedoms that they now enjoy.

Today I have a lot more freedom in society than the women who have gone before me. I can work outside the home, I can speak on issues that concern me, and I can choose how I want to live my life. I see myself as equal to men, and many women of my generation do the same.

However, we are still influenced by our upbringing and the beliefs and expectations of our parents. Many of us haven't learned to break free. Inequalities still exist in powerful positions and there is still often a disparity in salaries between the sexes. The 'glass ceiling' definitely exists and although many women do break through this social barrier, many more are held back from positions of prestige and authority simply because of their gender.

As women we also judge each other, often quite harshly. How many of us have learnt to break the shackles?

We adhere to society's expectations of us, we still hold fast to our roles, and there are often many of them. We identify with being a mother or businesswoman, a teacher or engineer, an artist or nurse. These are all fine professions, but we are more than our titles.

Now I'm not saying that there is anything wrong with roles. They have a place and they have a purpose.

They shape us, define us, and help ground us. They give us an identity as we step into life. They help us grow. They are a part of us, but there comes a time when we start to yearn for more. When we are ready to do this, we need to step out of the parts we play. We need to move beyond them to find out who we really are and who we want to become.

So why do we resist? Why haven't we learned to step out instead of hiding behind these guises?

Why do we steadfastly hold on to the masks we don, the ones we have been brought up with and were encouraged to wear? At a time in our lives when we have untold freedoms, why do we cling to these personas that were decided for us?

If we truly looked at the roles we take on, we may find that they are not necessarily empowering. Some of them may feel that way, but very often they take away from the essence of who we really are.

Yet we still continue to take them on.

They give us security and a foundation in life. They help us meet obligations or satisfy the needs and expectations of others. In fact, many of these roles place an incredibly high burden on us and ultimately can lead to failure.

We grow up believing we need to be someone or do something. We long for a purpose in life and take on a role that seems to fit. There is nothing wrong with that.

It is a starting point.

Sometimes these roles are necessary. They help us to survive, to navigate through our childhoods, to establish a career path or help us gain employment, or to support our families. Often our professions and who we become in life are influenced by our early up-bringing and may cause anxiety and distress.

Many others give us great pleasure. We may relish them for a while but are scared to move on. We find some roles all-encompassing and then start to lose the joy they once gave us.

But what if we explored the possibility that we are more than our roles? What if we found the very essence of our soul, our true essence, the thing that brings us great fulfilment and joy?

What if we were able to step out of these roles and become extraordinary?

What if there was more to us than living an ordinary life?

What if we were able to let go and fly?

That's what I set out to discover.

To receive your complimentary Book Bonuses, please visit

judynewbery.com/
book-bonuses

The biggest adventure
you can ever take is
to live the life of your dreams.

OPRAH WINFREY

CHAPTER ONE
Roles

The car came to a sudden halt. We were thrown back in our seats, straining against the seat belts. I couldn't understand what had happened. I pressed the accelerator and as we started to move, we were jerked forwards and then back again, before the car stopped. My sister, Cathy worryingly asked, 'What's happened?' 'I don't know,' I said. 'Something's wrong with the car.'

I was anxious as I drove in erratic stops and starts, across the car park onto the road. What was going on? I was driving my sister's car and had been feeling nervous anyway, but now I didn't know what was happening. I could feel her tension, and it only added to my fears.

I was in a strange car in an unfamiliar town, concerned about my sister and feeling quite stressed. Why couldn't I drive? As we were turning onto the road, a frightening realisation suddenly hit me. My sister's car was an automatic, unlike my manual one. Oh my God! I had pressed the brake, thinking it was the clutch.

What was wrong with me? I had never done this before. Driving had always been easy, no matter the type of car, automatic or manual. What was happening to me? I kept my thoughts silent. I thought I was losing it. My sister didn't need to know. She could see I was distressed and offered to take over, but as she was recovering from surgery, I knew this wasn't a good idea. My driving seemed the lesser of two evils.

I eased the car onto the road, and we made it home. I collapsed on the bed. My chest ached and I vaguely wondered if I was having a heart attack, but I was too tired to move. I just lay there, exhausted. I had never felt this empty and tired before. If this was what it felt like to be run over by a truck, then I was there. Completely depleted.

I realised that something was seriously wrong and that frightened me. I had always been able to think clearly. The episode in the car park had terrified me. What was happening to me? Why was I so tired?

I eventually arrived back home depleted and exhausted. A day's rest should fix it, I thought. A week later I was still struggling, and I knew things had to change. Fatigue had been creeping up on me for some time, but I'd ignored it. Certain tasks took longer to recover from. Exercise tired me more than usual and I woke up every day feeling unrefreshed.

My local doctor did blood tests but when everything came back normal, I was told I was just doing too much. Rest more. Do less. Reassuring in some ways but totally disheartening in others. I wanted answers.

Perhaps I could change my business hours and the way that I engaged with clients. So, I started to cut back the days I worked and had buffer days to recover. At first this seemed like a great idea, but I soon found that this wasn't enough. It wasn't sustaining me.

I needed to reassess the way I was living. My life needed to change. Things could no longer stay the same. But where to start? How could I suddenly find more energy? I had no idea.

Gradually, I began to look at the part I'd played that had led me to this moment. What was I doing wrong? What could I let go of? What changes could I make? Where was I giving away my energy and power? It seemed to me that I was giving and giving without realising the consequences. I had read a little about self-development. Maybe it was time to look more deeply into it. Maybe it was time to focus on me and me alone.

I began to look at the roles I had taken on throughout my life. Perhaps they had led me to this. It was a starting point.

I began to do some research and genuine soul searching to see just where I fitted in. Who was I? How had my family, childhood, and career influenced me? How had women's roles throughout history influenced the roles that I had taken on and the society that I had grown up in? Did the past have any influence on me or our freedoms as women today? I set out to do some digging.

Woman. Warrior. Princess. Mother. Daughter. Witch. Priestess. Feminist. Sister. Queen. Lady. Bitch.

Women have been called an assortment of names and have had various titles assigned to them throughout history, both flattering and derogatory. We do it ourselves. We take on roles throughout our lives and we assign each other names, even if they are temporary. How often have you called someone a bitch? It's very easy to label someone or put them in a certain category.

I found that the roles of women have changed dramatically over the past few centuries, when not so long ago, women didn't have a voice. Women answered to the names and titles they were allocated, such as Wife, Mother, Lady of the House, or Servant and have lived within the confines of the walls created around them. They were not recognised for their strengths or even acknowledged for them. After all, women had always been considered the weaker sex.

During the Renaissance period, a time from the fourteenth to the seventeenth century, women were very subservient to men. This period brought about a change from medieval times into a more modern age with huge artistic, cultural, economic, and political advancements. However, women remained beholden to men and were measured by their ability to give birth.[1] It was said that a woman's ability to produce an heir was "her only indispensable contribution."

Hence a woman's life was defined by motherhood, and this took up many years. A cycle of childbirth, followed by nursing the child, and then further childbirth ensued. For wealthier women who rarely breastfed, the cycle of birth was a constant. If the mother survived, very often the child did not. Grief, fear of their mortality, and a sense of duty consumed their lives. A son's birth was always more celebrated than the birth of a daughter because he could bring more wealth and fortune to the family.

I cannot imagine my life's worth being defined by the number of children I produced; having one child myself, I would have been delegated to a life of vilification and criticism. My "indispensable contribution" would have been minimal. I would have been finished, destroyed, with no hope, beyond redemption. What a terrible way to define your life. And yet that was what many women endured.

While men were defined by their roles such as philosophers, lawyers or physicians, women were defined by their sexual roles. Virgins e.g., nuns, or married women and widows, or girls who were yet to assume any role. A woman was expected to marry and social life did not allow for any aberrations unless she became a nun. A woman's role was defined by her relationship to a man, both economically and sexually. A man's role was to lead and a woman's role was to obey. A woman's place was in the home, as a daughter, wife, and mother.

Despite the advances made during the Renaissance period in terms of culture, education and the economy, it was very difficult for women to avail themselves of the benefits that this new era presented.[2] Women who stepped out of these norms were condemned by society. Any increase in their writing or speech was considered a threat to these traditionally male domains.

Although this period introduced new thinking and the expression of new ideas, women continued to live within the confines of their societies. However, the possibility of change was forming.

By the eighteenth century, things were slowly starting to transform.[3] Women were still answerable to their parents and husband and still had to endure multiple pregnancies and the risks of childbirth. However, in a period known as the Age of Enlightenment or Age of Reason, women started to have a voice. This era saw the development of an intellectual and cultural movement that emphasised reason over superstition and the emergence of science and logic over tradition and religion. This led to many social and political changes. The status of women and what it meant to be female were being disputed.

Women were beginning to question their roles as slaves and being totally subservient to their husbands. They began to take more pride in raising their children as the next generation of citizens, but the opportunities available to them depended very much on their position in society.

By the nineteenth century, the idea of marriage becoming a partnership that was based on respect and love had started to become popular but in reality, marriage was still an economic arrangement.[4] Women enjoyed only a few of the rights we take for granted today, such as the right to vote, and they had very little control over their personal property after marriage. Everything they owned belonged to their husbands and they were prevented from entering institutes of higher education. Their choices of occupation were very limited and dependent on their status in life. Middle and upper-class women generally remained home, caring for their children, and running the household.[5]

Birth rates were beginning to drop, and women's roles weren't solely centred on mothering but on developing skills in housekeeping and domesticity. These roles became more recognised with the publication of books on raising children and running an efficient household. These were perhaps the first "how-to" books that so many of us now refer to, albeit in a more antiquated form. Lower-class women, however, did work outside the home but usually as poorly paid domestic servants or labourers in factories and mills.

Divorce was uncommon and extremely difficult for women. Men had the right to divorce their wives on the grounds of adultery, but married women could not gain a divorce, even if their husbands had been unfaithful. If a divorce did occur, the man gained custody of the children and the mother could be prevented from seeing them.[6]

By the twentieth century, women's rights and education began to increase. As divorce became legal, many chose not to stay in loveless marriages. Women were choosing not to marry and have a vocation or find work instead and gain financial independence.

And they weren't burned at the stake!

However, women were still expected to choose between having a family or a career. They couldn't have both. Men were expected to provide financially to support the household and this concept carried through much of the twentieth century.

This century saw vast changes in the roles of women from the early 1900's to the 1990's.[7] and many of these roles were shaped by two World Wars. Women were finally given the right to vote, more and more women gained an education to improve their chances of employment, they became more involved in politics and finally in the 1970's.[8] gained access to an equal minimum pay.

Women were finally having a say in how they lived their lives.

It takes courage to grow up
and become who you really are.

E.E. CUMMINGS

CHAPTER TWO
Growing Up

The first role we all take on is in childhood. We are the new babies, the daughters or sons, the welcomed and cherished ones, or the unexpected and sometimes unwanted ones. This then starts to shape our early lives.

Being loved, welcomed, and given affection shape all of our physical and mental development as a human being.[9] Consequently, the roles we take on in our later lives, our competencies, how literate we are, whether we turn to crime. and even if we get physically ill have their roots in early childhood.[10]

Scientists have shown that the pre-frontal cortex, which they call the social brain, does not develop automatically. Rather it is formed in response to our social interactions as babies. The emotions and stress responses that we experience as adults are created during infancy. The brain develops through experience.

Hence the roles we take on later in life are obviously influenced by our childhoods.

I know mine certainly were.

My parents were born in the period between the First and Second World Wars. This influenced their values and beliefs and affected how my sisters and I were brought up. The confines of their generation impacted mine. My father was the head of the household, and my mother deferred to him as the man of the house.[11] This title also means the lord or master and that's how many men like my father expected to be treated. It was a cultural and generational belief.

While many women remained at home or worked part time, the male was the main income earner, so they expected to be treated with deference. His opinion and decisions were usually final. My mother was considered the weaker sex and although she questioned some of the family dynamics, she was still a product of her generation. Women were the housekeepers and owed their husband allegiance and respect.

Divorce was becoming more common,[12] but not for strict Catholics like my parents. So many couples put up with unhappy marriages or else accepted their roles in life. This was how life was meant to be.

I was one of three girls growing up in a sprawling old Victorian house in the inner Melbourne suburb of Thornbury. It even had a name, Scotsburn, a nostalgic link to the distant homeland of a previous owner. Having a house with a name was considered quite unique and upmarket in those inner suburban city streets, where houses were usually identified by a simple number. Thornbury was a working-class suburb then, a mixture of Australian and migrant families.

Having a name instead of a number was unusual and the name was never used. Perhaps my parents wanted to fit in or perhaps it wasn't important. The house had what today we would call character. It needed many repairs. The paint was always peeling on the faded white weatherboards, and the grey slate roof had seen better days. An array of buckets would line the hallway during any torrential rainstorm.

The bathroom was old with a hot water system that needed to be lit with a match every time you wanted to take a bath or shower.

You would turn the gas on, grasp the lit flame, hold your breath, and jump back.

Just in case.

It fired up with a huge whoosh and we were always terrified that maybe one day it might just blow us up along with it. We allocated this job to our mother until we were old enough to do it ourselves. It wasn't because we wanted her to be blown up, but we thought she had a lesser chance of destroying the house than we did.

There wasn't any room for a toilet inside this small bathroom so, as young children, we had to head outside to an old wooden hut at the bottom of the garden. It was surrounded by overgrown vegetation to provide some sort of concealment and harboured an assortment of spiders, hopefully none that were poisonous. Each evening before bed, my sisters and I were led down by our mother. Once it became dark, there was no way we would venture outside. After some years, a more modern facility was built at the end of our outside porch. Although this was a vast improvement, it was still too cold to visit on a winter's night, and we consequently developed strong bladders.

The kitchen had a similar hot water service, but the pilot light was always on, probably because it was the most used room in the house and was always full of warmth, my mother and company.

There was a wide verandah that circled most of the front of the house and provided shade in the heat on those long summer days. We often lay out on make-do beds on evenings when the heat became unbearable inside. The verandah provided some relief with the bonus of an occasional breeze and the singing of cicadas as a background chorus. Eventually numerous mosquito bites overrode our need for cooling down and drove us back indoors.

At the end of the verandah was a French window, which gave access to the sitting room. This was mainly opened to let in some air on warm days and otherwise out of bounds. Hence it held extra appeal for us. The sitting room was an elegant room where we weren't encouraged to play. It was kept for visitors, special occasions, and it was my grandfather's domain.

Climbing through windows was even less encouraged. However, my sisters and I would sometimes sneak through this window to avoid walking around the long way through the garden to enter the back door of the house. The front door was reserved for visitors.

It was through this window that we believed the angels delivered our Christmas tree each year. We knew this for a fact because we carefully followed the trail of pine needles from the side gate all the way to the locked window. It was one of the joys during this Christmas period that built up our excitement for the big day. The main door to the sitting room was also locked at this time and opened by the tinkling of a small silver bell that miraculously appeared on Christmas Eve. This was the signal to queue up outside with great anticipation for what lay behind those tall wooden doors.

In the colder months, the house was draughty and cold. The days of central heating hadn't hit our city, and most older homes weren't insulated. We spent many winters running between rooms that were heated by coal fires or electricity, avoiding the chilly hallways and only venturing out of our rooms when necessary.

The kitchen where Mum was always to be found, was the warm centre of our home. It was where we laughed and cried, helped shell peas, and prepare meals and fought over whose turn it was to wash up. There was always an aroma of something cooking.

Usually, there was a warm soup or the traditional roast on Sundays. We loved the spaciousness of our home, evident in the sky-high ceilings with intricate rose cornices, the large bedrooms with open fireplaces that were rarely used, and the long wide corridors that were perfect for running up and down or practising those ballet moves. We didn't mind the worn carpets or peeling paint or the ceilings that bore witness to leaks and pouring rain. It was our home, and we didn't know any different.

In the back garden was a two-room cottage where my uncle and aunt lived for many years before finally buying their own home. They owned the first television to grace our lives, and we spent many an afternoon visiting them to watch the black-and-white images on the screen. What a treat this was.

Our house was surrounded by a beautiful garden tended to mainly by my grandfather. My maternal grandparents had emigrated along with my mother and her siblings, and they lived with us. They gave us stability and wisdom as we were growing up and a safe haven to escape to when our parents just didn't understand.

Our grandfather had taught us how to play chess and the patience that goes with it. He was a former judge, and his wisdom and strength shone through in his words and actions.

Despite his education and former status in life, he was a humble man. Arriving as a refugee, he was willing to take on any work he could find to help support his family. At a time when most men of his age were considering retirement, he found a job in an automobile factory, a far cry from his expertise and previous profession.

He found peace and tranquillity in the garden. We had lemon, orange, and grapefruit trees and an abundance of fragrant roses framed by deep purple lilacs, wisteria, and sweet-smelling cherry blossoms. It was a sight to behold, as a carpet of pink fragrant flowers covered the grass underneath her outstretched limbs. The heady scent of lilacs and honeysuckle filled the air and the wisteria draped her long fingers, touched with purple flowers, over the old, corrugated shed.

A large brown owl would visit our garden every year and would sit in the high branches of a tall evergreen tree that hung over the garden shed. A gentle hooting would greet us in the late evenings, and its huge eyes shone out in the gathering dusk.

Our garden was the perfect setting for games of adventure that fuelled our young imaginations. We hid among the tall green bamboo and made cubby houses, where we played games of house and held tea parties. We climbed trees of all shapes and sizes. The taller the better. We rode wooden stick horses and galloped over makeshift jumps. We felt invincible. We raced each other on tricycles with the odd stop sign to create some semblance of control or possibly more chaos.

My sisters and I were happiest when left outside to play. My older sister, Cathy, was the fiercely independent one, questioning everything. She was the leader, the brave and fearless one. My younger sister, Sue, was the baby who had a few allergies, so she was always protected. She was incredibly sweet, the one who kept the peace and taking sides when needed so you never felt left out. She was, however, adventurous and unafraid to forge her own way. I was the middle child who had to find a pathway between the other two. I was sensitive and shy with a vivid imagination. I was a dreamer, a creative who loved writing stories and poems, and was quieter than my sisters.

I was kind and caring and generous. I didn't quite know where I fit in. Perhaps none of us did and we soon conformed to our parents' expectations of us. My older sister was outspoken, so she was always in trouble and considered the troublemaker.

She was a natural leader, but she was criticised for her voice and questioning views. My younger sister assumed the role of the baby so was over protected and had to fight to be recognised. I found my role as the good girl, the quiet child who was always well behaved and demanded little attention.

So, I gave up an undiscovered part of me that longed to speak out or misbehave and occasionally be naughty or even say what I really wanted. I wanted to be a rebel, but I didn't know how. I was too scared of the repercussions. My father had a bad temper, and I feared igniting it. If I behaved, I was safe. If I gave no reason to be criticised or admonished, I was praised. I was scared to make mistakes because if I did, how could I fit this mould of the 'perfect' child. This became the pattern of my adult life.

I would work extra hard, study more, and earn more qualifications so that I would be prepared for any eventuality. It's only now as an adult, that I can look back and see what an impossible burden I was placing on myself. To set out not to fail, immediately sets you up for failure because the outcome is unattainable. It's only when we make mistakes that we learn.

My voice remained hidden and small. Yes, I had a voice. I still spoke with my parents and sisters, but I rarely shared my needs or my views.

I saw my shyness as a weakness. Why couldn't I be more like my sisters? It was only many years later as an adult that I could see my sensitivity and shyness for what it actually was: a superpower.

I learned that if I assumed this role, in exchange I would receive praise, acceptance, rewards and validation. I took on this role with a frenzy, stayed quiet, and was well behaved. I allowed others to receive attention and always took a step backwards, effectively killing that part of me that longed to break out.

I surrendered my voice to those who were louder than me. I surrendered my growing soul to those who said they knew better. I vanquished those magical yearnings and the deeper parts of me that longed to break free. I kept myself silent. I escaped through playing games with my sisters and using my imagination to write stories. I wanted to be naughty, I wanted to assert myself, but I feared stepping outside of my designated role. I had to be responsible, so this meant staying quiet. It meant I had to be obedient. It meant I had to remain subdued.

I was afraid to be angry because my father was often angry. If I expressed my fears and concerns, I might upset him and trigger his anger, so I repressed my feelings to protect myself, my sisters, and my mother.

I was scared not only of Dad's temper, but of rocking the boat and altering the dynamics of my family. So, I stayed where I felt safe. Within myself.

In our individual ways, my sisters did the same. We became the versions of ourselves that fit in. We became the versions of ourselves that our parents expected of us until one day, we stopped. My older sister rebelled and moved out at the earliest opportunity. She questioned the status quo and today speaks up for justice and those who are disadvantaged. My younger sister remained at home for the longest time, but she eventually stepped out to forge her own way working with people with disabilities. I stayed where it felt safe, even if that safety compromised who I was until I, too, found my own direction.

While the garden surrounding our home was our escape and sanctuary, inside wasn't always so. Inside contained the laughter and love of my parents and sisters, but also the arguments and the anger and fear of a dysfunctional family.

Another member of our large extended household was my mother's brother, Elemer. While my mother's sister, Irene, was married and living with her own family, Elemer stayed at home. He was the youngest in her family, a shy and gentle man. He never married and at one stage, he planned to be a minister and dedicate his life to God. He turned to religion to fill his needs. He would often quote us passages from the Bible when we misbehaved, so we got into the habit of hiding from him when he was at home. He was close to my mother, but my father considered him interfering. He was often away on field trips related to his employment with the Melbourne Water Board and it was on one of these that he met a charismatic preacher who my sisters and I decided was the leader of a cult.

He began to spend more time away, lecturing us more when he was home and eventually, he started to give away his money. This caused great anxiety to my parents particularly when he wanted his share of the house. My grandparents had left the house to my mother and her brother in what seemed a sensible arrangement at the time. Elemer was single, unlikely to marry, and needed a home.

However, this change of events put great financial stress on my parents, caused many arguments and it led to my father taking on a second job on the weekends. Elemer passed away relatively young as he ignored his symptoms, believing more in the power of a preacher than his local general practitioner. We drove to the mountain village where his funeral was held, though we weren't made to feel welcome by his new friends. This convinced us even more that they were part of a cult!

Perhaps they were a normal church group but to my imaginative teenage mind, they were definitely weird.

> Fathers, be good
> to your daughters.
> You are the god and
> the weight of her world.
>
> — JOHN MAYER

CHAPTER THREE
My Father

My father was a controlling man who often found a household of women quite bewildering. If he assumed control, there was no chaos but if he let his guard down, we all ran free and wild. He lived by a very strict routine. Dinner was at 6 pm and couldn't be late or there was hell to pay. Meals were usually silent with only the occasional discussion, but controversy was never courted, and enthusiastic chatter was to be avoided at all times.

My father had his own seat at the table, his favourite cutlery beside him, and he controlled our television viewing. He was of average height, perhaps slightly shorter than other men of his age and had once been handsome as depicted in old family photos. He had blue eyes and blond hair and was neat and orderly in his manner and appearance. His actions were usually controlled and restrained, though he had an easy charm about him. He was a kind and caring man, but he did however have a temper and used this to enforce his will when situations seemed to be getting out of his control.

At night once we were in bed, we were expected to be quiet. Lo and behold if we decided to chat, as young girls who share a bedroom do, his voice would roar down the corridor and we would cower in fear. Mum would try and placate him, but this only fuelled his anger, so we would stay silent until peace reigned once more.

Dad, however, had a great sense of humour and loved playing jokes on us. He had a warm heart and would spend many evenings listening to my childhood stories or the latest poem that I had written. He took great pride in my achievements and those of my sisters. He was also a keen photographer and took many hundreds of slides of us in various positions sliding down sand dunes, playing in the ocean, and exploring rock pools. He was warm and loving, particularly on holidays when he could relax and leave his responsibilities behind. Perhaps the weight of them fuelled his anxiety and agitation. Laughter and anger lived uncomfortably side by side, in alliance with each other, until one became more prominent and ruled over us.

Each summer, we would go on an annual holiday to the seaside, and this in itself was a thoughtfully and strategically premeditated event. Everything was carefully planned out down to the organisation of the car boot. Everything we took with us, including beach balls and water toys, went into numbered boxes. These would fit into the car boot, according to a master plan my father had drawn up. No deviations were allowed.

My father's joy lay in his family, but his expectations of us were always high. He was very detail-minded, worked hard, and expected his girls to be the same. We were all bright and intelligent, so were expected to excel at school. This placed a huge burden on us from a very young age.

I often wondered what made him the way he was. His own parents divorced when he was very young, and he grew up in conservative Hungary without a father in his life. He used to tell us that his father had died when he was six years old. It was only when we were much older that we found out the truth. He seemed to have always been deeply ashamed of the divorce. His father apparently walked out on him and his mother, something that wasn't common at that time. His mother struggled to run the household and worked to keep food on the table, but she ensured that my father had a good education and a university degree.

The Second World War changed his life as it did for countless others. My father's first fiancée had been killed in an air raid and after the communists invaded Hungary, he decided to emigrate to Australia and start a new life. He planned to settle, then bring out his ageing mother. Arriving in Australia as a migrant and having to carve out a new life was not easy. He was intelligent and well-educated with a university degree, a PhD in political law, that wasn't recognised in Australia. White collar jobs were also hard to find. He started off his Australian life working in a gold mine in the small country town of Woods Point. Like many migrants, he took on whatever work he could find. Later he was able to secure a job in the city as a state trustee with the Victorian Government where his skills and intellect were in demand.

However, the White Australia Policy wasn't fully dismantled until the early 1970's[13] so discrimination against migrants was evident, particularly when it came to promotion in the workplace. The White Australia Policy was a name given to a collection of discriminatory acts in 1901 and 1903 that restricted the type and nationality of immigrants allowed to enter Australia. It was meant to protect Australian jobs and wages but was really a determination to keep Australia a nation that was mainly British in origin. It wasn't until after the Second World War, that a severe labour shortage prompted the Australian government to start relaxing some of its immigration policies and allowed more Europeans to enter. Discrimination continued in some form or other until the policy was finally dismantled in 1973.

Despite having more experience, qualifications, and knowledge than many of his work colleagues, my father was passed over for promotion many, many times. I don't know the exact reasons why, or if the White Australia Policy played a part, but he became more despondent and depressed, always struggling to make ends meet and provide for his family. He even took on a second job on Saturday mornings as an auctioneer selling houses. I'm sure this contributed to his decline. He suffered from arthritis and along with his physical discomfort, he became more and more withdrawn. He would later come home most nights with a bottle of whisky, his newfound companion.

Much of his life was out of his control, so perhaps his family was the only area where he felt he had influence.

Why is my father's story so relevant? Because his beliefs and experiences helped shape our household for so many years. I learned honesty, kindness, caring, and responsibility from both of my parents but I also took on their beliefs of playing small, working hard, perfectionism, and conforming. Perhaps it was post-war migrant tendencies or perhaps those of a father who felt he had missed out on life's opportunities, but he was determined his daughters would not do the same.

I also learned about the importance of family and the love and support they offered. Having a large extended family felt normal to my sisters and I. We shared many picnics, birthdays and Christmases with my grandparents, aunts, uncles, and cousins in the midst of so much warmth and love.

Today my family is still of utmost importance and the seeds laid down in childhood have grown into a strong sense of love, support, and companionship that family provides.

I often wondered about my mother and father's relationship. I knew they came from very different backgrounds and perhaps in another time, they may not have met or married.

Chapter Three » My Father

Mum's childhood was spent in comfort while Dad's was a struggle. They were poles apart in many respects and as a child I only saw their differences. Mum was the happy, impulsive one who was also a huge worrier. Dad was the more sensible, responsible, practical one. Mum was the one we went to when things were hard, or we needed advice or just a chat and a spontaneous hug. I would go to Dad for praise, maybe because he gave it out rarely or conditionally, so it felt extra special or even grander.

Each anniversary, my father would present my mother with a beautiful gardenia, a rare, perfumed treasure in the cooler climates of Melbourne. He would show his love in unexpected ways. Mum's love was always more apparent.

As we grew older, we tended to rebel against the constraints of our childhood and assert our independence. Dad couldn't cope with this and it led to many arguments. He started to withdraw even more. Eventually it was our brave, adventurous, impulsive mother who took us alone, on holidays to mountains and undiscovered trails, walking for hours in the bush or camping in the wilderness.

"Mother is the heartbeat in the home; and without her, there seems to be no heartthrob."

LEROY BROWNLOW

CHAPTER FOUR
My Mother

My mother had been brought up with a deep love of nature and God. She spoke many times of skiing in the Austrian alps and hiking in nature with her many cousins. She grew up in an affluent family in Budapest and her early childhood was very carefree. Her aunt and uncle were bestowed titles by the king and she often spoke of her aunt, Margaret, the baroness. Mum was very proud of her heritage. She studied to become a teacher and spent all of her summer holidays at the family holiday home in the mountains in the northern part of Hungary. She was a tall, slim woman with soft, wavy brown hair that she kept short and manageable. She had been brought up to be a lady, a role she adapted to with grace. However, she was a romantic and an adventurer, and these yearnings often clashed with her upbringing. She was imaginative with a great sense of fun, but she also had a deep sense of duty to her family and duty usually overrode her yearnings for freedom and adventure.

During the Second World War, she and her family had to escape the invading Russians, an event that stayed with her throughout her whole life. She would relate the fear and terror that the night had held and how lucky they were to escape safely to Bavaria.

After the war, she worked as an *au pair* in London to help support her family. She came out to Australia along with her parents and siblings a few years later and left behind her dreams and innocence. She lost her sense of safety, financial security, and her birth country. She'd had to navigate a new role that had been thrust upon her. She had been a school teacher in her native Hungary, but learned to speak English and became a nurse. Then roles followed as a wife, mother, homemaker, and the ultimate people pleaser. She was kind, warm, and loving and put everyone else's needs before her own. I certainly had a great teacher!

She was also a worrier, perhaps a trait she was born with or something she'd developed during the war. She tended to sweep things under the carpet rather than face them if they became too overwhelming. She also shared her imagination and love of nature and the beauty that could always be found around us.

Brought up with a housekeeper, she had never learned to cook. It was an art she had to quickly master once she married, but it never sat well with her. My father was a hard taskmaster and many attempted dinners ended in tears.

Eventually she learned to just cook whatever seemed the easiest and we became used to the overdone vegetables and well-done roasts. However, her cakes and strudels were the very best and a Christmas staple. My sisters and I learned the basics of cooking and adapted our own techniques as we grew older.

Despite not having a huge affinity for cooking, she filled her kitchen with her warmth and love. Many hours were spent talking about our latest boyfriends or bands we liked or our school homework. She was always there to listen.

When we were slightly older, my mum returned to nursing and we became latchkey kids. We would find the backdoor key hidden in the outside laundry and let ourselves in to a house that was chilly, empty, and devoid of her presence. Nothing felt normal until she returned late in the evenings to light up our home and dispel the cold.

Our own adventures with her took us up to high mountaintops where we hiked for hours, never really sure of where we would end up. We did get lost occasionally, but this was all part of the adventure. We saw stunning mountain vistas and drank from cool, pristine streams. We saw flowers and plants we had never seen before amongst the snakes that occasionally crossed our path.

We saw kangaroos, koalas, echidnas, and a huge variety of birds in the wild. We went camping in small two-man tents and enjoyed campfires and sang songs. Mum, however, was a real lady through and through. Even while camping, she wore dresses or skirts with stockings, then, later on, pantyhose. While my sisters and I lounged around in the briefest of shorts and halter neck tops, she remained true to her upbringing. It was only on extremely hot days when we swam in mountain streams that she dared to take her stockings off and have a paddle. The Victorian Alps, especially Bright, was a favourite spot where we often returned, along with Wilson's Promontory. It was at the latter that we bodysurfed and learnt to navigate rips, went on long walks around pristine bays, and played in the soft, white quartz of Squeaky Beach. The sand really did squeak as you walked on it!

My mother was such a free spirit when she was allowed to be herself and have fun. I don't think she allowed herself to live this life when the responsibilities of motherhood and running a household took over.

At home she assumed her role of the dutiful wife and caregiver. It was only on these trips in nature that we saw her true self. She gave my sisters and I a glimpse of our souls, the fun, adventurous part of ourselves that we usually kept hidden. She instilled in us a love of nature, travel, and adventure that became lifelong passions for all of us. Her sense of fun and curiosity and the ability to laugh at herself and the world kept her youthful well into old age.

She gave us a very precious gift indeed.

> There is always one moment in childhood when the door opens and lets the future in.
>
> GRAHAM GREENE

CHAPTER FIVE
Childhood Roles

How many of us were assigned roles as children? I certainly was. We send our kids to ballet and football lessons. We get them to join clubs, learn a musical instrument, and take up hobbies. Sometimes they want to join in, but sometimes they are dragged kicking and screaming to the next dance class, music lesson, or sporting event to become more social or active.

Are we as parents really conscious of our children's desires or are we fulfilling an unmet need from our own childhoods, where we were never given the opportunity to dance or swing a bat or to sing ourselves? We rarely ask ourselves this. We so often just encourage our children with vague undertones of manipulation. 'I never had the opportunity. You will love it'. 'It's so important to be social. You'll make more friends'. 'Give it a try. You might love it. We can always leave if you dislike it'. How many times have we used these words in an effort to appease our kids? I know I did the same.

Despite my best efforts to only encourage my son to do the things he really wanted to do, we attended many painful violin lessons long past their use-by date. I ponder now on how I would do things differently if I had the chance. Would I allow my son to make his own choices or would I still try and influence him, believing that as an adult I knew better and could guide him? I'm not sure. The ego is a powerful adversary. It keeps us safe but also holds us back from allowing ourselves and others to have true freedom.

My forced activity was the Hungarian Scouts, a combination of male and female scouts. My sisters and I were dropped off each Saturday morning to Westgarth Hall, an old community hall in the neighbouring suburb of Northcote. The building was dated and didn't have much furniture, with an ancient, functioning kitchen and an assortment of odd chairs. There we would learn how to tie knots, repair broken arms, learn Hungarian history and how to dance the csardas, a Hungarian folk dance.

To a painfully shy child, these regular visits were a torment. I was particularly shy with boys and later, as blossoming teenagers, we were forced to mix regularly. I was the quiet one, the one who kept to herself, and I wasn't witty nor could I come up with some speedy repartee. I found it painful to share my thoughts and speak my mind. I had had little practice after all.

We had no choice in this matter. It was part of our education, perhaps a link back to the motherland for our parents. It was their way of educating us about their culture, which in itself was worthwhile. I just wish it had been done some other way.

Every year we would also attend a camp spent in the bush in what is now the outer suburbs of Melbourne. At the time, these outer suburbs were untamed bush with few houses and acres and acres of undeveloped countryside. Being young, I felt lost away from home. My sisters and I were put into different groups and I felt alone. We would go on long hikes with heavy backpacks in the searing summer heat. Perhaps this was to teach us resilience. I'm still not sure but at the time, it felt as if we were being tested for an Olympic marathon.

Over time, I made friends and grew within myself. I became stronger and more resilient and gained some invaluable insights into the Hungarian culture, insights that have served me later in life. One of the greatest benefits of this experience was continuing to learn and practice the Hungarian language, no small feat indeed. Hungarian has been said to be one of the most difficult languages to learn. It is not related to its European neighbours but rather belongs to the Finno-Ugric group of languages, which include Finland and Estonia. My early induction stayed with me and though I'm a bit rusty, I can still speak the language today.

Sex and religion
are closer to each other
than either might prefer.

THOMAS MORE

CHAPTER SIX
Sex and Religion

Religion plays a powerful role in many people's lives and it often shapes the people we become. Religion is one of our strongest belief systems and it binds communities together or, in some instances, tears them apart. Many wars are fought over religion and friends and neighbours may become enemies. It can be inclusive but equally divisive. It can lay the foundation for our lives, bring comfort, love, and peace but can also cause anger, anxiety, and pain.

My sisters and I were brought up strict Catholics with the spirituality and the guilt that this entailed. We attended weekly Mass and regular confession, said our evening prayers, and were educated by nuns in Catholic schools. They instilled in us duty, belonging, values, guilt, and a strong sense of fear. Doing the right thing was all that mattered. Sin was everywhere. If we were bad, we would need to repent or the gates of Hell awaited us. If we were good, the path to Heaven was open. We were taught that the Catholic religion was superior to any other. Our God was the only God and we were told to have pity for the Anglicans who knew no better.

This was confusing and made me question how many gods there actually were. Why was mine superior? Was it because He was a Catholic too? My grandmother was a Catholic but my grandfather was Presbyterian. Their daughters were raised

Catholic while their son was a Presbyterian. I often wondered why, as the only son, he was given such an inferior calling.

So much of what we were taught was based on fear. There was a right way of doing things and a wrong way. If you ever ventured towards the wrong way, you would pay dearly. In primary school we were told that God was calling us to follow Him. Boys were encouraged to become priests and girls were encouraged to become nuns. I took this literally. Maybe it was not meant to be taken that way, but some of the nuns that taught me certainly believed this. There was nothing more noble than following a holy path. I was terrified that God would send for me to be a nun. I had no idea how he would contact me, but I feared I would one day get a message. Perhaps it would be a phone call or maybe even a letter. I couldn't think of anything worse and for years prayed, "Please don't let me be a nun. Please don't contact me." As I grew older and no letters or phone calls ensued, I felt I was safe.

Confession was another traumatic event. This happened on a regular basis at primary school or before religious events such as Easter. We had to line up on cold, uncomfortable, wooden pews in the local church and wait until it was our turn to step into the confessional box. This was usually an ornately decorated wooden structure inside the church with a room in the middle for the priest and doors leading to a cubicle on either side, for the person confessing. When it was your turn, you entered and knelt before a little shuttered window and shut the door behind you. It was dark, intimidating, and slightly musty inside. When the priest was finished with the person on the other side, it was your turn. He would slide back the little window to give him a slight view of you and then ask you to confess your sins.

As a child, I didn't have too many so I felt I had to exaggerate. 'Forgive me, Father, for I have sinned. It has been…(insert days/

months/years) since my last confession." The longer it had been since your last confession, the more penance you usually received. I would then say things such as, 'I disobeyed my mother, hit my sister, was angry with my father, etc'. Sometimes I couldn't think of anything so made something up. Then I could add, 'I lied'. I felt this gave me extra kudos. All trivial things were made to feel like crimes. I was then given ten Hail Marys to say as penance to beg forgiveness from the Lord.

These occasions further enhanced the fear and guilt around religion. If God was indeed a loving God, then how could these events be reconciled. They only created more anxiety in an already impressionable child. Perhaps if others like myself were taught not to fear and feel guilt, more people would not have left the church.

Today I have the insight to see past these teachings and have my own relationship with God and spirituality. My God is indeed a loving God who I chat to when I want and I have no fear or guilt around my beliefs. My thoughts and beliefs are not necessarily shared with the Catholic Church but that's okay. It took me many years to realize this, however, and feel comfortable with it.

Interestingly I bought my own son up in the Catholic faith. Why did I bestow this role upon him after my own upbringing? After all, my husband wasn't Catholic. He was an Anglican. I felt that my son needed to be given a belief in life as a grounding for his future. Also, he needed to follow a superior religion.

Just joking.

Whatever path he would choose later in life was up to him but I wanted him to have some faith. My husband was happy for our son to be brought up as a Catholic and fortunately the church is more open now and his education wouldn't be based on fear.

Tied up with religion was sexuality.

Like many of the Catholic Church's teachings, sex was sacred, an act only to be performed in marriage. I was taught little about sex at school and even less by my parents. It wasn't something my parent's generation discussed, but my mother felt it was her duty to give us some sort of sex education. As sex was something that only took place once you were married, my mother tended to gloss over the details. She was too embarrassed to discuss it fully so there were vague explanations with a lot left to the imagination. My sisters and I learned more from our friends and each other than we ever did through any so-called expert on the subject.

Even more taboo was sex between the same gender. This was considered perverse and wasn't even mentioned in our household. I can only imagine the fear around coming out as a gay person in the seventies. How hard it must have been to recognise your feelings for another but not being able to express them. The stigma was enormous and had far-reaching consequences. Certainly, the Church condemned homosexuality and, as a result, most Catholic households did too.

Sex was always discussed in hushed tones, even amongst my sisters and friends. Although I knew of my sisters' boyfriends, even amongst ourselves, we never discussed what took place. We were too shy and sex was always considered taboo. We never discussed each other's exploits. Sex was an embarrassing subject.

My parents never discussed it either and we rarely saw displays of overt affection between them. There was the quick kiss on the cheek, a hug, or a kind word but nothing more.

Occasionally they would disappear into the bedroom on a weekend afternoon, telling us they were taking a nap.

Curious as always, we girls would creep up to their bedroom door and try and peek through the keyhole to see what was really going on. The key was, however, in the lock so we only ever saw a black void. They must have heard our whispered chattering outside the door since we were very quickly sent on our way, none the wiser.

The warnings concerning sex centred around pregnancy. Sex led to pregnancy and unless you were married, it wasn't okay. The contraceptive pill was available but only through your local doctor and the family GP who had known me since childhood was not a suitable confidant. Hence sex was best avoided, at least for the time being. Sex was also a part of our religious upbringing. The Catholic Church prohibited sex before marriage and this was drummed into us as children. Although we were no longer so conforming, fear still lingered around sexual relations. Certainly on my part.

I was shy with boys and felt uncomfortable with my feelings. I enjoyed physical contact and touch, but I was scared where it would lead. My indoctrination had been thorough and I feared pregnancy.

I eventually met a man I loved and my fears were allayed, but I think back on all the opportunities I missed and how much more fun I might have had.

A friend is someone who helps you up when you're down, and if they can't, they lay down beside you and listen.

**WINNIE THE POOH
BY A.A. MILNE**

CHAPTER SEVEN
Friendships

Friendships are the relationships we choose. They play an important role in our life and I believe, are one of our most important relationships.

Our first friendships are often those formed within our own family. Interactions with our brothers, sisters, cousins, other relatives, or neighbours of a similar age are usually our first experience of making friends. We have friends over for play dates and although we may argue with our siblings or our neighbourhood friends, it's through play and arguments that we learn to share, become allies, trade secrets, learn skills, and gain companionship[14]. We learn affection for each other and form our first relationships outside of the ones we have with our parents. My sisters were my first friends and although we often argued, we also laughed, cried, played games, and formed a lasting bond with each other.

As we grow through childhood, we tend to form friendships with those who have similar characteristics and interests to us. My first best friend was a girl at my primary school called Janilla. We were inseparable, sitting next to each other in class, playing games together and getting into trouble together. We were taught mainly by nuns and their views on punishment and reward were very questionable. Janilla still recalls us both scrubbing the black and white tiled floors of the next-door convent. We considered it a privilege to enter such a holy place! We would visit each other's homes and learn about our different cultures. My family was Hungarian whereas hers was Italian. Although we drifted apart for a time as we grew older, those first few years of having a best friend were invaluable. My first friend outside of family was very precious. Thanks to the wonders of social media, I was able to pick up those threads of friendship after many years.

When we are children, friends can also be transient. "You're not my friend anymore!" is a common cry when we fall out over some minor transgression. We can be friends with those we care about or those we share games or hobbies with. Sometimes we invite others into our friendship group out of kindness. When I was around eleven or twelve years of age, I invited a girl to my birthday party. She wasn't one of my usual friends, however I felt concern for her. She was disabled and appeared to be lonely.

Like many children in my class, I had little knowledge of disabilities and society was less inclusive then. I somehow wanted to show this girl that I cared and that she shouldn't feel left out. We stayed friends for some time after the party until she changed schools. Friendships are meaningful and we may never realise how much a simple friendship means. It enriches both the giver and receiver.

Once we are adults, our friendships remain an integral part of our lives, particularly as women. They become deeper, more intimate, bring us joy, companionship, and provide an anchor in our lives. They can be a source of great happiness and transformation and are great for our mental health[15]. Our girlfriends are our confidantes, the ones we share our deepest fears, dreams, and secrets with. It is with our true friends that we share just who we are without any need for pretence. It is with them that we feel safe and we're able to share our true essence. It is these friends that we reach out to when we need advice.

Over time, our friendships vary. Some people have large friendship groups that form an integral part of their social networks. Others have smaller groups of friends, couples, or individual friends that they closely relate to. I know that I am the latter. I love my friends but enjoy more intimate conversations with them on a one-on-one basis.

Friendships may change too and this is a natural part of growth. We form connections with others at different stages of our lives to meet a specific need. This may be at school where we learn to socialise, or through a career where we share common interests or goals. As we grow, our interests and our friends may change. What we once had in common may no longer seem important. We may move on and make new friends.

Friendships are deep and complex relationships. They can cause conflict when you disagree and cause pain and disappointment when you feel that your friend has let you down. This too can be a part of growth and a realisation that your companions are human too and just as fallible as you are. Sometimes a friendship may become unhealthy where there is jealousy or manipulation involved. These so-called friends need to be let loose and cut free as they only serve to undermine our own self-worth. True friends will always be there to boost you, guide you gently when you need it, and support you with a deep sense of affection and caring. These are the friends we need in our lives.

We may find that our closest friends are our partners or husbands. We may see them as a soul mate or someone who deeply understands us. This can be found in friends outside of partnerships as well and it's important to nurture these friendships. Friends outside of your intimate partnerships help you stay connected to others[16]. They provide an avenue for shared interests, give you a different perspective on life, and encourage independence. If you are open and allow yourself to be vulnerable with those who you are closest to and the ones you love to spend time with, you will find a true affinity with them.

I have been lucky enough to have made some wonderful friends throughout my life. Some have been transient, made though my travels, whilst others have been more enduring. Some have lasted through schools, careers, and through my own son's school connections. All have given me so many lessons of love, kindness, true fun, laughter, and a sense of self. We often take our friends for granted. They are always there. But just like any other relationship, friendships need to be nurtured. They take time to establish and more time and effort to maintain. However, the rewards are immeasurable. True friends are those where even after many years apart, you pick up the threads of conversation and love, without any effort.

Being a friend, being there for others, sharing of yourself in all your vulnerability and receiving love and acceptance in return is one of the most precious gifts in life. The role of friendship cannot be underestimated and although this role may change and develop over time, it's something that's quite indispensable.

When you see a role model, what you see is a person who has the courage to be who you wish you could be. Stop wishing and just be.

ANONYMOUS

CHAPTER EIGHT
Role Models

The roles we take on in life are influenced by our role models and our first role models are our parents or those who raise us. They form our beliefs and outlook on life until we are old enough to make our own choices and decisions. Our mothers are said to have the most influence on the first three years of our life due to our need for sensitive nurturing and bonding[17]. Our fathers are said to have a really strong influence from the ages of five to eight as they demonstrate role-modeling behaviour and play just as the child becomes aware of their own control and power[18].

As we reach our teenage years into young adulthood, we look to other role models outside of our family. These may be teachers or relatives we look up to, celebrities, or athletes we admire. How many people take up tennis after watching a major tournament?

Many teenage girls fall in love with members of the latest rock band and want to emulate them. I know I did. I had posters of my favourite bands or their lead singer on my bedroom walls and attended as many rock concerts as I was able to go to. I still do, though I no longer have a crush on any performer. Well, maybe secretly!

Why do we follow these stars that we know very little about and rarely have a chance of meeting? Why do we need role models?

Role models serve as examples. They inspire and influence us to be better or different versions of ourselves. They show us how to behave, make decisions, and form relationships[18]. They often show us a more exciting life or a different way of living. We may not necessarily want to live their lives, but they show us a glimpse of the possibility and allow us to dream. We usually admire them and look up to them and often want to copy their behaviour or learn from their own experiences. We may see them as our heroes and people we want to emulate. We often put them on a pedestal.

In my teens, I followed various bands and had a crush on many of the band members. I would attend their shows and knew all of their songs. Many teens would dress like them to show their devotion. It was fun and exciting. It gave us all a sense of belonging.

When I commenced my nursing training, one of my role models was a qualified nurse that I worked with. We got on really well. She was capable, had a great sense of humour and drove a sports car. I wanted to be like her. She was a positive influence in my life and encouraged and motivated me to be a better nurse. Although I looked up to her and followed her guidance, I never did end up with a sports car. Maybe that would come later.

Why do role models have such an impact on the adults we become? Because they have a powerful influence on our behaviours and beliefs. Society is full of various role models, some good, some bad. The actions we display and the lives we live are based on the role models we encounter throughout our lives.

They give us as sense of identity and help shape us into the people we become. They inspire us to try new things, experience more in our lives, and discover more of what makes us who we are. They help us to rise up when we need motivation and support us when we are feeling discouraged.

Not all role models are beneficial as some may exhibit inappropriate or anti-social behaviour. Just look at the tabloids that feature the negative antics of a famous film star. Also, if our parents are negative role models in our formative years, we may exhibit their behaviours later in life.

I believe that it is important to acknowledge role models and their contribution to our lives, but it's not really beneficial to put them on a pedestal and make them out to be someone they are not. Despite their attraction, fame or celebratory status, they are still human beings and not machines. Often, we expect them to live up to impossibly high expectations and we then criticise them when they fail.

Role models give us ideals to aspire to, but they need to be recognised for what they are. We still need to be accountable for our own actions and take responsibility for ourselves and not always seek their approval. We can thank our role models for their contribution to our growth, and acknowledge them for their own frailties, fears, and anxieties.

It's also vital that we remember to be our unique selves. We can take on all the education and information we need, but to find our true essence, we need to look deep within ourselves and find out who we really are.

I had yet to do that.

Do not go where
the path may lead,
go instead where
there is no path
and leave a trail.

RALPH WALDO EMERSON

CHAPTER NINE

Family

As I grew older, I followed the path set out for me. I was expected to have a proper job and a career that would give me stability and financial certainty. Things that both of my parents had lost after the war. My imagination craved creativity and a job in the arts, but my parents were adamant. An artistic career had no stability. There was no guaranteed income. There were so many so-called "starving artists." Why waste my education and my intelligence? A proper job would give me security. The arguments were many. As the good girl, how could I resist? My programming had been too successful. I was the ultimate people pleaser.

What then is a people pleaser? It is someone who not only pleases others, but someone who fails to please themselves. They put everyone else's need first. Others take priority over themselves. Others needs are always more important. This is what I mistakenly told myself over and over again. This, however, wasn't true.

Unless it's an emergency or an urgent health issue, others don't need to come first.

You do!

It was many years before I learned this. As a young eighteen-year-old, I was keen to please my parents, so I listened to their advice and a career in nursing followed. I thrived in this caring role and enjoyed being able to help others in their healing. It felt good to be able to provide some reassurance when so many lives often hung in the balance. However, I was still the little perfectionist and gave totally of myself during every shift I worked. As a result, I was often put in charge of the ward when no senior nurse was working. The charge nurse would say, "We can always depend on you." This placed enormous pressure on me not to make any mistakes and get it right. No wonder I had so many sleepless nights and felt sick every morning before work. The lessons of childhood still lingered.

Nursing defined me yet again, but it gave me independence and the freedom I craved. I could do and go where I wanted without the approval of others, particularly my parents, and I had my own earnings to spend as I wished. I travelled extensively, using all my savings on holidays. At work I still assumed the role of the good, responsible girl, but on holidays I was exploring my boundaries. I was becoming a woman but unsure of my place in the world.

It's interesting how careers define us or how they allow us to define ourselves. We label ourselves as a nurse, teacher, doctor, street cleaner, shop assistant, lawyer, etc. They are jobs we do, but they are not who we are. Society creates labels, which in turn create assumptions about us. This then creates expectations. Caring professions are usually looked at with respect and a certain type of behaviour is then expected to follow. A nurse is considered compassionate and caring and is expected to behave in such a way. A parking inspector is looked at with disdain and suspicion even though he or she is just doing a job. We are very quick to judge others because of the title or role that they have taken on.

Roles, however, do have some benefit as we usually use them to orientate ourselves. They are a compass in our lives when we are starting out or discovering where we want to be and what we want to do in the world. We strive to be a certain person depending on the beliefs we have taken on in childhood. These same beliefs may also instill a fear of becoming like our parents. We see their mistakes and rebel against becoming like them. Very often we don't realise that we are just repeating the same mistakes ourselves. Beliefs can be difficult to shake off and unless we are aware of that, our behaviours end up reflecting them.

Travel not only broadens the mind but it helps you to find out who you really are, as you usually have no idea as a twenty-something year old. When I began that wonderful experience of travelling, I certainly didn't. You've been let off the leash and now you test your boundaries. You don't know who you are yet or what you are capable of. You experiment and try out different things.

My travels took me to Europe, Tahiti, the Pacific Islands, and many cities around Australia. A whole new unimagined world had opened up for me. I was hooked. My first trip to Europe was with a close girlfriend on a Contiki tour, which included numerous countries over a six-week period. Living on a bus with a group of other excited young adventurers can be exhausting, but I made some lifelong friends and it was fun!

It was also an opportunity to be silly just for the sake of it. To really let my hair down and be me without judgment or criticism or any adult telling me what to do. There were also no expectations of me. After being responsible for everyone else as a nurse, this was such a welcome relief.

One of the funniest things we did as a group was an activity called Dead Ants. Someone was nominated each day to call out these words and on hearing them, the whole group would drop to the ground, lie on our backs, and shake our arms and legs in the air like dead ants. This was only effective if done in a public place and gained extra points if performed somewhere well known, such as in front of the Eiffel Tower, at an airport, or going through Customs. At a time when airport security wasn't as stringent, we were fortunate to get way with such silliness.

Buoyed on by my fellow travellers, I tried paragliding and riding a moped rather badly in Corfu and came home with a myriad of bruises. I drove across the Nullabor desert in southern Australia with a group of girlfriends in an old camper van that broke down in the most unexpected and deserted places. I rode on the back of motorbikes in Tahiti with some Australian guys we met and cruised up breathtaking, stunning fiords in Norway. I also conducted the orchestra in the Munich beer halls (I must admit, after having a few unfamiliar beers). Not bad for someone who is tone deaf!

Travel builds character. It opens your mind to a new way of living. It shows you other cultures, food, and places you never imagined existed. It can be scary and terrifying, but it can be incredibly rewarding. You make lifelong friends, fall in and out of love, create memories, and have fun like you never knew you could. You also discover parts of you that you didn't know existed. The fun and silly parts, the freaking terrified parts, the panicky I-can't-do-this parts, and the amazingly resilient parts.

These experiences set me up for life. They gave me a foundation of what was out there beyond my normal realm and far beyond my comfort zone. It showed me and continues to show me every time I travel that there are incredible people out there, amazing places to see, and fantastic food to be discovered and eaten. Every time I travel, I also grow in confidence, knowledge, and humility. I certainly don't know everything and there is a whole wide world out there for me to experience and learn.

Chapter Nine » **Family** | 55

At the age of twenty-one, I visited my parents' homeland of Hungary while it was still under communist rule. I was on my own, young and adventurous. Budapest appeared grey and austere, far removed from the vibrant capital city it is today. I had to report to a police station within twenty-four hours of arriving, stating all my details, where I was staying and with whom. However, I was greeted so warmly by my mother's relatives and I rapidly became one of the family. They lived in a small village with unmade dirt roads. Oxen ploughed the nearby fields. The scent of dust and farming filled the hot summer air and I felt as if I had stepped back in time. Their home was modest but overflowing with warmth and love.

Life was not easy, but I came to realise what strength the amazing Hungarian people had and I was really thankful for the freedoms I had at home. I saw the places my parents had walked, from the majestic mountains and verdant pine forests to the university towns and medieval villages. I saw a glimpse of the lives they had left behind and the families they wouldn't see for many years. I discovered a family that I, too, had on the other side of the world. I was their connection to a different world, one my parents had discovered in the name of freedom.

When do we break out of our childhood moulds? Do some of us remain entrenched and imprisoned or do we all eventually break free? I had generally followed my parents' guidance but longed for the freedom to make my own life choices, the ability to decide what to do and make my own mistakes. Travel gave me this freedom.

When I was twenty-three, I went to Africa. I had grown up watching Daktari[19], a television show about a vet and his daughter who looked after orphaned and injured animals. These included a chimpanzee called Judy and a cross-eyed lion called Clarence. We see shows on television and dream of being kissed by a handsome prince or flying off on a magic carpet or living in some remote and exotic location, but these TV shows are often far from reality.

I didn't want to adopt a lion or have a pet chimpanzee, but I was fascinated by Africa and decided to go there one day. A girlfriend and I planned our trip. We were going to hire a car and visit all the well-known sites like Kruger National Park, the Drakensberg Mountains, and the iconic Table Mountain. However, our well laid-out plans never materialised as my friend pulled out due to family reasons, so I was determined to go it alone!

My mother was horrified.

Some British, American, and Australian tourists had recently disappeared near Victoria Falls[20]. South Africa was still under Apartheid rule and it was no place for a single young woman on her own. Computers, email, and mobile phones were unheard of so all she would receive were the occasional postcards.

I went anyway.

I left Melbourne on the long flight to South Africa via Zimbabwe. Due to the government's policy against Apartheid at that time, Australian airlines weren't allowed to fly there directly so I flew into Harare. I arrived, feeling a bit sick and tired and thought it was due to the long flight. This wasn't helped when I had to stand in the searing heat on the tarmac waiting to enter the airport terminal, surrounded by soldiers with machine guns.

Eventually, I entered the coolness of the dim arrival hall to await my connecting flight to South Africa. Imagine my delight when a familiar voice called out to me across the rows of seats. It was a girl I had met in Europe a few years previously and we eagerly exchanged our contact details in Johannesburg.

After arriving in South Africa, I checked into my hotel room and collapsed onto the bed. I felt really ill and wondered what I had eaten. Perhaps the prawns on the plane weren't such a good idea after all! Whatever it was, I spent the next few hours in the bathroom. I felt terrible and suddenly scared. Here I was in a strange country on my own, worried, ill, and not knowing what to do. I was due to leave on a tour the next morning so I tried to ring the company, but it was after office hours and they were closed. Mobile phones were yet to be invented and the internet was still unavailable to most. I felt very isolated and panicky.

Suddenly, I remembered my friend from the airport and gave her a call. Hearing a friendly voice on the phone made a world of difference and I felt a lot more confident. She suggested I ask the hotel to call a doctor. Why hadn't I thought of that? A few hours later, a doctor arrived and diagnosed me with food poisoning. An injection stopped the vomiting and I was able to leave on my tour the following day.

Africa was an experience that changed my life. The vast beauty of this old and mesmerising land can't fail to touch your soul. It was wild, with many areas seemingly untouched by man, herds of wild animals, breathtaking sunsets, and that sprinkling of danger that made you feel alive. I felt a huge sense of freedom in these vast landscapes that spoke to my young adult heart.

The sight of majestic elephants crossing the dirt roads in front of me, sleeping under the stars in a campsite in the wild near where lions roamed nearby, being charged by a magnificent elephant when we got a little too close, the ancient wisdom in the eyes of a rhinoceros, or the graceful leap of antelopes fill every moment of my waking day. I swam in rivers downstream from crocodiles, where it was safer to have a dip, explored the Okavango Delta in dugout canoes feeling a part of that huge landscape, spent ten hours travelling only one hundred kilometers on corrugated dirt roads, and saw the magnificence of Victoria Falls and the oppressed lives of those under Apartheid in South Africa. African sunsets imprint on your soul.

I also met my future husband, a funny, charming English man who captured my heart.

At first, I ignored him.

He was funny and often the centre of attention. He had an easy charm about him which I mistook for cockiness. He was older than me by nine years. He smoked a lot (like my father). This was enough to put me off, so I tried to avoid him.

Yet I was drawn to him. He was good looking with dark brown hair and warm blue eyes, had an easygoing nature, a sense of fun, and an inner confidence that I didn't possess. He was nothing like my previous boyfriends, perhaps because of his age and maturity. I was twenty-four. He was thirty-two. And he was attracted to me too. We both had very strong feelings for each other, but I hesitated. Was this just another holiday romance? How could it amount to anything more? I was scared to commit.

On my return home, he wrote to me and said he was coming out to Australia. I panicked! What if I didn't like him anymore? What if it was all a disaster? What if he expected more than I was able to give? I still didn't trust myself or my feelings. I told him not to come. He missed my letter and luckily ignored my fears and came out anyway. Two and a half years after settling in Australia, we got married.

My husband worked in the corporate world, an alien planet to me. I was introduced to a concept called 'entertaining clients', something totally foreign to an introvert like me. I was not the life of the party. I preferred to chat with one or two friends in a quiet corner. I was sensitive and friendly but found it hard to force conversation with those I didn't know. I did, however, love the dance floor so if there was any dancing, I was in.

Entertaining clients was a totally new concept. Making small talk with strangers was terrifying and unnerving. If we had something in common and clicked, then that was great, but all too often the conversations became forced after the "what do you do? How many children do you have?" type of social niceties were over. If any deeper discussion was initiated, it was rarely welcome and quickly quashed. The main bonus was going to the opera, ballet, and tennis events that were always welcomed. They partially made up for the feared new people I had to socialise with.

These events also made me question what was acceptable in a particular social setting. When we go to a party and meet someone new, we usually introduce ourselves. Then we usually ask what the other person does as a career. What work do you do? What sort of job do you have? Or else they may ask, 'Do you have children? If so, how many? If not, why'? This is often followed by or an awkward pause. I have one wonderful son but I still get asked, 'Did you only want one'? Do you want more?" Yes, I did, but it was none of their business.

How many of us have done that? How many of us have asked these same questions? These so-called social norms orientate us to who people are in life and give us judgements on how they live. These preconceived judgements are usually wrong but we pride ourselves on having conversations and being social.

What if instead we told them about our real selves? What if we said we love nature and spend our time outdoors or that we are creatives or artists or write books? Would they still be interested? Would they think we were weird? Would we be brave enough to share more deeply of ourselves? Would we be scared of criticism, or worse, rejection? Or would people think we are strange and judge us anyway? Either way, people usually have an opinion. Does it really matter what it is? If not, then why not be more open and truer to yourself or are we too scared to shed our masks?

Motherhood is the biggest gamble in the world. It is the glorious life force. It's huge and scary – it's an act of infinite optimism.

GILDA RADNER

CHAPTER TEN
Mothering

Three years after our wedding, we welcomed a beautiful son into our lives. Life felt complete. I was a wife and a mother. I slotted neatly into these roles, believing they now defined who I was. I didn't question where my true self fit in. I didn't have the awareness then. I was happy and felt I had achieved a life's goal. My own family. We would do things differently and I would raise my son in an open-hearted, loving way.

Little did I know that I couldn't leave my beliefs and upbringing on the doorstep. They only persisted in accompanying me inside.

I stopped working when my son, James, was born and later returned to working part time. I threw myself wholeheartedly into motherhood. I was made for this. I was in my element. The people-pleaser, the good girl, the caring perfectionist. I was determined to always be there for him, this beautiful innocent child. I wanted him to know that there would always be someone supporting and loving him for who he was and that I wouldn't try and influence his decisions the way my own parents had done.

We grow up adhering to rules. They are important and give society structure. We obey road signals, we respect other's properties, we don't rob banks (hopefully), and respect the lives of others. Without rules, there would be anarchy.

However, not all rules are equally important. Some of them are based on someone's interpretation or society's norms. Society places expectations on how we should raise a child but what we actually end up doing can't be found in any guidebook.

Parenting is often about instinct—what you know is right for your child. Obviously, we are guided as first-time parents, for example, when to introduce solid foods, start toilet training etc, but these rules or guidelines don't define our roles as mothers.

What does it mean to be a mother? Mothering means to nurture and it comes in many forms.

It may be the actual process of giving birth or being a mother to another one's child. It may be showing up as a stepmother, a mother to our pets, or simply mothering ourselves. It's the sleepless nights, the fears around your child's illnesses and falls, the responsibility that you have taken on, and the questions you repeatedly ask yourself. "What have I done? How am I ever going to cope? What do I do now?" It's the anxiety when they are late home from a party, or driving their first car, going on their first date, or the million and one reasons you question your answers and judgement. It's also the joy of that first smile, those first words, the best of hugs, that little hand holding tightly to your own, the unquestionable trust that they place in you, and discovering a love deeper than you ever imagined was possible.

As a new mother, we often take on the role with gusto as I did, but it's easy to forget that mothering ourselves is equally important.

By being the so-called perfect mother, I didn't realise how much of myself I was leaving behind and how much I was holding my son back. I was always there for him, supporting and encouraging him. He was a shy and sensitive child and I totally related to that. I "got" him. I thought he was so like me. He was, however, his own person, and I had to learn to let go and allow him to grow into the man he would become. Holding him back only caused resentment and eventually he would break free.

Control comes in many forms, the games you let your child play, the people you let him or her mix with, the schools you choose, the clothes you expect your child to wear. You encourage independence while holding a lead so that you only let him stray so far. You encourage free thought while giving your strong opinions and think that you know better. Raising a child is tough, especially when you believe you are doing a better job than your parents. You are the better mother because you don't think you judge, you are the better parent because you encourage communication, and you are a better role model because you allow your child to be themselves.

This, however, comes with conditions and one of them is do it your way, but only so long as I approve.

You don't realise that you are making mistakes like your parents. You just make different ones.

How can you be a great role model for your children when you are still figuring it out for yourself?

How can you guide them on the best path to take in life when you are still unsure of where you're headed or if the path you're on is the right one for you?

You don't know.

You just do the best you can at the time. As you learn more, this may change and hopefully you haven't stuffed it up too much the first time. Let your children see that you are human. You make mistakes and are allowed to make mistakes. That's how you grow. Let them make their own mistakes too. Let them find their own path in life.

Ignoring my own needs was not a good lesson for my son. It was only later that I realised that the best lesson I could have given him was to know that I was human too. As such, I could make mistakes, I would make them, and that it was okay to have my own life outside of motherhood.

I chose to be a mother. I embraced that role. I loved the privilege of being a mother, for that's how I saw it, but I forgot that my own needs were equally as important. I sacrificed myself along the way. I forgot to honour who I really was. I had gifts and talents that I wasn't using. I had dreams and expectations and visions for my own life, but I never allowed them to come to fruition. They were put in that ever-increasing, bursting-to-capacity basket called Later.

I'll do it later when he has finished school.

I'll do it later when he leaves home.

I'll do it later when I'm not working.

I'll do it later when Mum or my husband doesn't need me.

I'll do it later when I have more time.

I'll do it later when I have more energy.

Later never comes.

And what of the many women who can't have children despite desperately trying for years? Or the ones who decide they don't want children. Or those who lose a child. How do our roles change then?

If you have always wanted a child but can't have one, be it because of infertility, body clock, waiting to find the right partner or the right time, a broken relationship, or the myriad of other reasons, where then do you sit in the world?

If you have your heart set on being a mother, then how do you find your compass? Do you redefine your place in life by continuing the roles you had taken on previously? Do you throw yourself into your career more wholeheartedly or should I say, more "wholeheadedly," as heart rarely has anything to do with it? Or do you look into your heart and see what the rest of you really wants? The part of you that hasn't had a voice. The part of you that knows there is something more, despite that aching void. The part of you that has to reevaluate your life and knows there is still an abundant life to be found, albeit in a different direction.

I am not in this category, though I did desperately want more children. I told myself that I was lucky to have one and yes, I was. But I had family and friends that had to renavigate their lives when they weren't able to conceive and it was heartbreaking.

What of the women who choose not to have children at all? Life choices, circumstances, careers, and past trauma may all pay a part and there is nothing wrong with this choice.

In the past, women who were childless were called spinsters or, if married, they were considered barren. What a horrible term. Barren brings up images of a dry, dusty, bleak, and lifeless landscape. Hardly descriptive of a living, breathing vibrant woman. They were shunned, shamed, or pitied for circumstances that were out of their control or because of their own free choices.

Religion and cultural norms expected women to reproduce and it was frowned upon if a woman opted out. She could be ostracised from her community, was considered selfish, called a nun or prostitute, or infertile even if she'd chosen to be childless. Single women in the 1600s were even suspected of witchcraft and hanged for the offence.

Research sociologist Jean Veevers in her book *Childless by Choice*[21] says that many women quote freedom, the time to concentrate on their relationship, and the ability to have a lifestyle that they choose as reasons for not wanting children.

Today women have more choices and many decide that motherhood is not for them. They choose careers, freedom to live life on their terms, and a financial independence that their mothers may not have had. As historian Rachel Chrastil says, "Childlessness and parenting are both part of the unfolding human condition."[22]

That's not to say that childless women always put themselves first. A career or demands from family and friends may still take precedence. Motherhood or a life without children still can place us in roles defined by society. We may still take on roles that are expected of us. I don't have children so I can work longer hours, I can be more available as I don't have to do school pickup, I can take on more responsibility since I don't have commitments at home.

Choosing not to have children doesn't necessarily mean that we have true freedom to choose our lives. It depends on what we choose to emphasise as most important.

Motherhood is another role that we can choose to take on or can be denied it when we want it so badly. We may also choose to decide against it. And that's okay.

> Her absence is like the sky, spread over everything.
>
> C.S. LEWIS

CHAPTER ELEVEN
The Night The Stars Went Out

Life has a way of throwing you in the deep end and testing your strength and I never realised how much mine was about to be tested.

One cold, wintry evening, a phone call changed all of our lives.

My brother-in-law's voice was on the other end, stark, shocked, and emotional. My younger sister, Sue, had collapsed and stopped breathing. She was resuscitated and in intensive care in a country town many miles away.

I made a call to my mother with the pretence of another work function to attend with my husband, to spare her the shock of driving to my home while distressed. She came over to mind our son, thinking that her youngest daughter would soon be transferred to a larger Melbourne hospital. Therefore, she decided to stay, babysitting alone, and praying through the night that her youngest would survive.

It was a long drive through the unrelenting, pouring rain. Unfamiliar, empty roads were made more foreign by the dark, wet, cold conditions and diminished visibility. The country town was a two-and-a-half-hour drive away. Why did she live so far away? As I cried, feeling scared and alone, I began to reassure myself that she would be okay. She always was. I felt cold, sick, nauseated, desperately praying. She had to be okay. Where was God? Could he hear my prayers?

We sat in the Emergency department, waiting and feeling powerless. Empty, silent hospital corridors devoid of all life, at that late hour. I was terrified and felt confused and desperately afraid.

The consultant arrived. His words washed over me.

No hope. Massive brain haemorrhage. Brain dead. On life support. Only resuscitated because of her age. No hope. She was only thirty. No hope. No future.

Turn off the machine.

Time to say goodbye.

Crying, numb and in shock, we left the hospital in silent despair. There weren't any words for the emotions I was feeling.

Driving home, still numb, the tears seemed never-ending. Seeing Mum on our arrival, there were even more tears. Then, there was the matter of telling my older sister when she came home from a camping trip. I was holding the family together and barely holding myself together. We were trying to hold each other tighter together and trying to support each other. The whole time I was squashing my own feelings. All the while, there were more tears. More sorrow. No words. Just a deep, dark heartache. Innocence lost.

Looking at the night sky with my mother, I sought answers amongst the Milky Way. The sudden noise of a possum in a tall dark gum tree alerted me. Was it a message from Heaven or just a disturbed night creature? Perhaps just wishful thinking, as I hoped and prayed to a starry sky.

Finally, it was the day of the funeral. Hundreds were there. It was a blur of a day as I stood there, numb to it all. Jim Croce singing 'Time in a Bottle'[23] still breaks my heart.

Chapter Eleven » The Night The Stars Went Out

The light has gone out and nothing can restore its brilliance.

No more Susie singing 'Thunder Road'[24] or dancing to Bruce Springsteen's music. No more Susie to hold and hug. No more Susie to laugh with. No more Susie to grow old with.

That night a part of me died. That light, indomitable part of my soul that had told me I was invincible. The part that believed in miracles. The part that filled me with indescribable joy. That lightness of spirit and that absolute joy in life. I didn't know if it could ever be retrieved or if I wanted it to. I was suddenly vulnerable and scared. I had never lost someone so close to me before. My grandparents had both died when I was young but since they were elderly, and I had mourned them, I could justify their loss. Sue was only thirty!

Our son was two and I had to keep on going, but I was numb and felt empty. I had lost my direction and I had no compass or navigational skills. I floundered and cried. A lot. I sought answers, but no one had any.

Sue had epilepsy. Maybe it was related to that. Maybe it was the contraceptive pill. They suspected that, but no one could tell me. The doctors didn't know. Would it have made any difference? Could I have rationalised it then?

I saw a priest and a counsellor, but their platitudes and offers of solace fell on deaf ears. I wanted my beautiful, free, lively, caring sister back and no-one could help me. Even my mother, who followed God fervently, began to question His judgment.

Four months later, my father died. He had had dementia followed by a stroke and after that, he barely recognised us. We saved him the knowing of Sue's death, protecting both himself and us from his grief.

Another funeral. Another loss. With this one, I felt like a passerby. I was still numb, untethered. Lost and grieving, I supported Mum without any anchors for myself.

I coped by holding those close to me even closer. Death was at the door. I had to keep it out. If my husband was ten minutes late home from work, the train had crashed. If he was late back from some errands, he had died in a car accident. If he didn't answer my calls immediately, he was dead or had been taken ill. If my son had a cold, it was pneumonia. If the phone rang, it was bad news. Who else had died? I was scared to answer it. I was scared of knowing and I was even more terrified of not.

We all experience grief at some time in our lives but when it's unexpected and sudden, it's hard to understand and even harder to accept.

I had lost my compass, my orientation in life. Before everyone was well and happy and life was great. Now I had to redefine joy and meaning in my life again. My two-year-old son gave me purpose and a role to play. I could still be a mother and a damn good one. Giving him my attention grounded me, but it pushed my own sorrow deeper down and I ignored my own need for healing.

How can you know
what you're capable of
if you don't embrace
the unknown?

ESMERALDA SANTIAGO,
CONQUISTADORA

CHAPTER TWELVE
The Unknown

When our son, James, was four years old, an offer came up for my husband to work in England. He had wanted to move home after ten years in Australia. I knew I needed to give him the opportunity. We made the decision to move for his career and because I felt I couldn't hold him back. I knew he would never resent me if I insisted we stay in Australia, but I also knew I would feel guilty. I was good at that. The ultimate people pleaser, I put his needs before my own.

It was a really difficult time in my life and the last thing I wanted was to leave my home. My younger sister had died two years previously, my father a few months after, and my mother-in-law a few months after him.

I knew my mother was still grieving, but I had to put my family first. I felt an enormous amount of guilt as I was taking her only grandchild 12,000 miles away and I knew she was most unhappy about it. But we went anyway, leaving my older sister and my mum behind.

How can you win? I felt guilty if I said no to my husband and guilty for saying no to my mother. We sacrifice our lives for the lives of others and we sacrifice our happiness, believing it's for the higher good.

Did I want to move 12,000 miles away? In all honesty, no! Did I want to leave my mother and sister? In all honesty, no! Then why did I agree? Because I was the dutiful wife, the people pleaser. Could I please my mother and sister? No, but I could please my husband.

Sometimes we have to choose the least distressing option. Which role did I want to play? Which role did I have to take on? As women, we so often choose the lesser of two evils. We play the devil's advocate to keep the peace. To choose the easier path. When doing this, we seldom consider our own desires or even stop to question what they are.

We feel we have to do the right thing, especially if we are playing the good-girl role. After all, aren't we being kind and considerate and thinking of what everyone else wants? Isn't this how we gain love and praise? Doesn't this validate our existence? It certainly did for me.

I felt very anxious moving to a new country and navigating an entirely different way of living. There was an excitement about a new adventure but a fear about coping and getting it right. My husband's family was warm and welcoming, but they left me on my own.

While my husband commuted to London every day, I learned to navigate a new way of life. Banking, shopping, local doctors and health care, kindergarten, and later schools were all different. It was a very lonely time. I set up a new home for us, took on some part-time nursing, found my way around some seriously frightening motorways, and kept myself very busy.

But I was lonely and missed home. I missed my mother, sister, and the friends that knew me. I never realised how much history matters.

The friends who have known you since primary school or the ones who have walked beside you through all your growth, failings, and successes matter and they had never mattered more. When friends spoke about seeing old schoolmates or university friends, I felt left out. No one knew my past and it mattered to me. How could they be true friends if they didn't know that I had been head girl at primary school or wrote poems to which a friend added music, or that I loved dancing until the early hours, or that I once had too much Mateus Rose?

How could they share in my experiences with me when they had no idea about them? Eventually, I would make friends who welcomed this girl with the strange accent and no past. They accepted me for who I was now and that was enough. Together, we formed new experiences. Perhaps it was only me who felt that the past mattered. It took time but I started to settle down, though the warmth and sunshine of Australia still felt a million miles away.

I had never thought much about the class system in England, but it became more evident when our son started school. It started with accents, which apparently determined where you were from. There was the more affluent south, the poorer north, or somewhere in between. Though it was never spoken out loud, you were subtly judged on this, as well as where you lived or the clothes you wore. It seemed to happen particularly in the private school system. I fell into no man's land since I had neither a class or accent that could be predetermined. As I was Australian, I was a bit of a novelty and accepted by both sides. This was to my advantage as I got to see who was really genuine and those who just wanted to know the new girl.

I was incredibly fortunate to make some wonderful friends who just wanted to know me, regardless of where I was from. I learnt a lot about acceptance and false values. I also learnt a lot about precious friendships and speaking my truth. I also learnt that not everyone wanted to hear it. The more reserved English sometimes questioned the thinking of a more outspoken Aussie.

My mother came to visit on numerous occasions, the first time being when I had fallen down the stairs and broken my ankle. It was lovely to see her flying over to rescue me but, in the end, I was unsure who was saving who. I had had an operation and my foot was in plaster, yet I still had to look after her as well as the household. We argued once when I told her she was selfish and she was shocked that I had talked back to her. 'I never spoke to my mother like that', she said.

Perhaps I was finding my voice and finally speaking up for myself. Maybe not in the right circumstances and I probably could have put it differently. It did, however, clear the air and so I felt it was warranted. I had to learn to put myself first.

It was also an opportunity for Mum to see her family in Hungary. She had only been back one time since she left so many years ago. Seeing her family was always very special. My husband, son, and I travelled around the United Kingdom and had many wonderful holidays, both there and in France. These were fun family times. No pretences, no need to be anyone else than yourself. A time to appreciate the beauty of nature and the history of such old and venerable lands.

We settled in a one-hundred-year-old cottage in a small village near the Ashdown Forest[25], an area of open heathland and ancient woodland. The forest dates back to Norman times and was once a medieval hunting forest where deer still roam.

It remains the largest area of free open space in South East England. It is also where the beloved book, *Winnie the Pooh,* was set and that was what held the most attraction for us.

Chapter Twelve » The Unknown

We discovered the beauty of the English countryside right outside our doorstep with lots of adventures and walks into the nearby forest. We explored places such as Pooh Sticks Bridge, where we threw sticks into the fast-flowing creek to see whose stick would come out on the other side first. Most days, we walked up old bridle paths and sandy walkways to reach higher areas with outstanding views of the Sussex countryside.

We also discovered a special place we named the Secret Garden. It was a part of an old estate that had been reclaimed by the forest, with winding paths, tall beech and oak trees, and small lakes. There was also an overgrown long neglected garden with stone bridges and the occasional herd of deer. We accessed it by walking across stepping stones over a very small, shallow creek and then entered the garden through an old wooden, moss-covered gate.

It was such a lovely garden. There was rarely anyone else there and if we were very quiet, we would often see deer. There were a few stone bridges to walk over and a little waterfall with a creek tumbling over some stone features, lined with moss and native flowers. There were lots of old rhododendron bushes flowering beautifully in the warmer months.

There were also three lakes, which once may have contained fish but now lay quiet except for the many dragonflies that hovered over. It was such a peaceful place.

When my son was small, I would tell him to keep a look out for fairies. The abundance of red-and-white-spotted toadstools fuelled our imagination. Didn't fairies live under them? We played with our walkie-talkies and hid amongst the trees, sending messages to each other, and we had many adventures there.

I made some life-long friends, discovered Reflexology, which would become my new career, and learnt resilience and just how strong and capable I was. We had some wonderful experiences and, although life was hard at times, I discovered just how amazing life could be when you allowed yourself to be open to new adventures.

We would end up returning home after a transformational eight years.

During another one of Mum's visits to see us, she took James on a walk to the Secret Garden. Relying on a young child for directions was never going to end well and they both became hopelessly lost. However, all the major paths led home and they soon found their way back. Mum was impulsive and often didn't think things through, but she had the best imagination. Our son adored her.

At school, I became the mother who was involved in everything. A volunteer was needed to help the children read? "Me, me. I can help." Helpers were needed for the school fete? "Me, me. I can help." Mothers were needed on the school committee? "Me, me. I can help." Both in England and, later, back in Australia, I threw myself into school life enthusiastically. My own mother had helped at school when she could, but I had more time and only one child. I had taken on this mothering role with gusto. I wasn't going to back out now.

School became a huge part of my life. Another role demanded by society. Another role encouraged by the school system. Yes, it was great to be there for my son and I know that he enjoyed me being there. Wasn't that enough? Didn't I have my own needs?

I had forgotten about my needs when I signed up for motherhood. They weren't part of the contract. There was no exclusion clause.

I learnt to identify with the roles I had taken on in life. If I didn't know who I was or what I really wanted, my roles gave me an answer.

I was a daughter. This meant responsibility towards family, belonging, selflessness and putting others first.

I was a nurse. This gave me a direction in life, a career to build on. It taught me empathy, patience, and responsibility. It gave me confidence in myself and what I could achieve. I was a wife. I learnt to love deeply, to share, to compromise, and I learnt the beauty of a deep partnership.

I was a mother. Motherhood had opened up a whole new world for me. The only person I could ever die for without hesitation. I learnt incredible joy, more patience, more fear and worry than I could imagine, an unbreakable bond and an indescribable love. Again, I learnt to put others first.

See the pattern?

I threw myself wholeheartedly into every role that I took on, but I'd never once considered my own needs. In not doing so, my voice stayed silent and small. A small flame burned within me, but it didn't know how to grow. It didn't know that it had the possibility of starting a huge fire. I effectively put my life on hold. Career, parenting, and family came first. There would be time to do what I wanted later. I could always write, draw, paint, and dance later. Others needed me now.

We can't be afraid of change. You may feel very secure in the pond that you are in, but if you never venture out of it, you will never know that there is such a thing as an ocean, a sea. Holding onto something that is good for you now, may be the very reason why you don't have something better.

C. JOYBELL C.

CHAPTER THIRTEEN
Letting Go

When do we learn to let go? Do we ever do this or do we fear entering uncharted waters? What would happen if we let go of total control? Would we drown or would we learn new ways of navigating the ocean?

I found myself thinking about the legacy we leave our children. What do we teach them about letting go, about growing up, about responsibility? Do we teach them to be authentic or expect them to mould into the versions of themselves that we would like to see? Do we encourage their independence or do we hold onto them tightly out of fear? Do we teach them to accept themselves as they are or do we hold onto those fake, impossible images we see in magazines?

I realised that I had a lot to learn. I wanted my own son to grow up to be his own person and to make his own decisions based on the premise of caring for himself and others. I knew that he needed to be independent, but this is easier said than done and it takes courage. Courage that I didn't know I had.

James moved out of home when he was twenty years old, not an early age you might say. It's something we all expect our children to do. We hope that we have brought them up to be independent human beings so that they feel confident establishing their own lives. But to someone who held on so tightly to all she could hold, this was devastating. The sudden decision to move out with his girlfriend totally floored me.

Since the death of my younger sister, I couldn't deal with sudden loss or dramatic life-altering decisions and this was sudden and dramatic, and life-altering for all of us. And it brought up memories of my sister's sudden loss and of a grief that I wasn't prepared for or expecting.

The ties that bind can be suffocating and my son needed to find his freedom. I needed to let go and trust him and his judgement. He needed to know how to navigate the world and I needed to learn how to navigate a home without him. His poor girlfriend had no idea of my feelings and I had no idea how to convey them to her or anyone else. I didn't really understand them then. I cried every night for months. I felt such a deep loss. If I wasn't a mother anymore, then who was I?

Logically, yes, I was still a mother but the emptiness he left behind was a huge gaping hole that would take some filling. I know that many parents find it hard when their children leave home, but I never realised just how difficult it would be[26]. The 'empty nest syndrome' is real and affects parents in different ways. It wasn't just my son's absence that I found difficult. It was the thought that I would miss out on so much of his life. His experiences, joys, sorrows, and growth had been such a huge part of my life for the past twenty years and no longer having this was painful. I knew I was going to miss the son that I loved. My identity as a mother, as a parent, was being challenged and I had no answers. How would he cope? How could he study and still pay the bills? How could he have chosen the girlfriend over his mother? This last thought shocked me. Was I that controlling or had I just given up so much of my own self to be a role model? To be the perfect mother. If I couldn't be that, then who was I? My fears were not just centred on our separation, but on suddenly realising that my role in life had changed.

These were my confused and emotional thoughts as I learnt to let go. I had to allow him to be capable and stop smothering him. I had to learn to let him be an adult and I had to stop playing the abandoned and controlling parent. His life was his own. It wasn't mine and he needed to live it without my interference. I didn't need to know everything that was going on in his life. By not knowing, I wasn't missing out. I was just allowing him to grow. It was a painful lesson to learn, but it was necessary for both of us. And guess what? He survived and grew within himself. He gained confidence and self-responsibility. He learned how to run a household, cook, clean, and pay the bills.

As we grow, the roles we take on may change and we enter uncharted waters. We either adapt or we fight against a rising tide, and that's a situation we can never win.

My husband and I had to discover a relationship that didn't focus on the three of us. The house felt empty and the household dynamics had certainly changed. It took some time to find ourselves again along with the love and the interests that had bought us together many years ago. We spoke more deeply to each other, went out more, and regained the spark that had always been there, but we had been too distracted by parenting and the needs of a third person to feel it. Our marriage strengthened because it had more focus. I began to focus on me and who I was without the title of motherhood.

James learnt freedom and a chance to be himself. He made his own mistakes and his own brilliant decisions and grew the wings he needed to create his own life. By cutting his own ties to home, he took back a power that I could possibly have never given him. He became independent in a way I could never have foreseen.

Though the relationship with his girlfriend later ended, he had learnt such valuable lessons about life and found out that he could manage on his own. He was learning to become his own person, not just a son, grandson, or nephew but a funny, bright, caring, and intelligent man with his own inherent sense of adventure. Later, he would move overseas for a number of years and although this was another wrench to the heartstrings, it was somehow made easier by the knowing that he would be okay. I had let him go and he had learnt to fly.

One of the greatest tragedies in life is to lose your own sense of self and accept the version of you that is expected by everyone else.

K.L. TOTH

CHAPTER FOURTEEN
Losing Myself

How can you lose yourself? It's not like losing a set of keys. You usually misplace those or put them in a drawer and find them after a frantic search. But you cannot do that with yourself. If you start to lose who you are, the quest to find 'You' is much more difficult.

Little did I know that small parts of me were being lost in the ether. I couldn't find these parts of me in a drawer, forgotten, or put away for safety. I was far more complex and I still had to discover which parts of me that I had actually lost or forgotten versus which parts I really wanted to find.

All my life I had lived by my beliefs and the expectations of those around me. I had taken on a certain role. I was kind and considerate of others, never willingly went out of my way to hurt someone, avoided confrontation so that myself and others wouldn't suffer, and tried to please everyone around me. I had never realised how exhausting this could be.

I said 'Yes' before thinking about whether I had the time and energy. I agreed to help those who needed assistance believing I should be there for them. I was sensitive and caring and didn't want to let anyone down. After all, my sense of worth had been formed by the praise I received and what I achieved in my life. I gave of myself until I had nothing more to give. And then I gave some more.

Fatigue is an insidious beast.

It climbs up on you slowly and stealthily while you are totally unaware. It appears to hide while you sleep and tricks you into believing that it has gone away. However, when you wake up and resume your day, it raises its ugly head yet again. Eventually, it infiltrates your night time too so that your precious sleep becomes even more elusive.

You tell yourself stories and then convince yourself that they are true.

"I'll go to bed earlier tomorrow. I'll have an afternoon nap each day. I'll do less on the weekend."

And you do.

And you feel a little better, but the day after that or the following week, you're back where you started. Tired. No energy. Pushing through each day yet again. You start to cut back on the things you enjoy just so that you have the energy to do the things you think you should enjoy. You make plans to see friends and family, you have long chats with your girlfriends on the phone, you take your child to school sports, you engage in life. But a part of you remains distant. You're hoping everyone says 'No'. You're doing what you feel is expected of you, but your heart isn't in it. You just want to curl up somewhere and hope the world goes away.

You know you can't keep going like this, but you can't see a way out.

I did all the right things. I saw my local doctor many times. I had blood tests and they were always normal. I was told to do less, rest more.

I cut back the hours I worked and accepted fewer social engagements. I thought that if I did less, I would have the energy to do more. I could take on a different role. The one of someone less engaged and less obligated. I began to reduce the things I enjoyed, thinking that I would be able to cope better. However, I was beginning to lose more of me, of who I was. The things that lit me up, that brought me joy, became a burden. Each time I went away on holidays, I would recover a little. I always came back feeling more energised and revitalised. My doctor said my fatigue came from stress. If I wasn't stressed, I would have more energy.

Although there was some truth in this, I still didn't know how I could change my situation. But I listened, I took advice, and I took up meditation. For those who have never meditated, it isn't an easy practice to begin. How can you stop a chattering mind when all your mind is thinking about is how to stop it chattering. I had read some literature about it. It couldn't be that hard.

I decided to make it manageable for me and began with five minutes of listening to a guided meditation while sitting in a shopping centre carpark after the morning school drop off. Hey, I was great at multitasking. Five minutes was up. Tick. I had completed my meditation. Tick. I was feeling less stressed. Not really. I just needed more time. Perhaps this meditation thing would take a while.

So, I went shopping.

> He who knows others is wise;
> he who knows himself
> is enlightened.

LAO TZU

CHAPTER FIFTEEN
Who Am I?

I had travelled interstate to see my sister, Cathy, and offer support while she was recovering from breast cancer surgery. She had had a serious health scare and needed an operation. She was living in Townsville, a regional city in the north of Queensland, far away from family. We'd always been close to each other, especially since we had lost our younger sister, and I wanted to be there for her.

I was terrified of losing another sister and I could only suspect how lost and frightened she was feeling. She was my brave and fearless sister, the leader of us three girls. To see her so vulnerable was terrifying and I felt lost and powerless. By this stage I was becoming more tired, yet I felt she needed me more. I had no idea, however, how much support I, myself would end up needing.

Then the incident happened in the carpark where I had forgotten how to drive. I didn't understand what was going on. Perhaps it was the emotional strain and worry. Perhaps I was doing too much. I had never felt so fatigued or scared and I vowed that once I got home, things would change. I didn't know how, but I knew that I couldn't keep going as I had before.

So, what do you do when you have no more energy? When you are so exhausted that you are bereft of thoughts and feelings? How do you go on? How do you make decisions that will lead you forwards? How do you keep up hope?

How do you know who you are anymore when all the parameters that defined you have shifted? What is your role in life when everything changes? When you don't have the energy to be that person anymore, the one who you thought you always were. The kind, sensitive, giving person. The 'good girl', the happy one who just got on with what life threw at her. The one who gave one-hundred-and-ten percent every time.

Perfectionism is exhausting!

No, I didn't have some life-ending illness, but I certainly had a life-changing event. This may sound dramatic but if you've ever felt that depleted of energy, you'd understand. If suddenly everything centres around your health, the decisions you make on an everyday basis end up being affected.

If I feel well enough, I will attend that event. If I have the energy, I will see more clients. If I had no health issues, I can do amazing things.

My health was holding me back! This was the assumption I came to. If I had my health, I could do anything, but if I didn't, my opportunities were limited.

I had been wrong. My health wasn't a perceived weakness in my body. It was a message to pay attention to it. I had taken it for granted for too long. It was time to listen to the nudges. By ignoring them, I was ignoring my health.

The body, however, doesn't give up. If you ignore the nudges, they soon become more insistent and even bolder. They speak louder. They become more obvious in the headaches, pain, and fatigue that make themselves known. They speak from your gut issues. They speak from your very soul until you finally pay attention.

Then the body finally heaves a huge sigh of relief that says, 'At last!'

I came to realise that my body was always sustaining me.

I realised that I could no longer keep living the way I had been. I had to live my life differently. I had been living a life where I thought I should be doing so many more things than I was currently doing. I should be doing more exercise. I should be eating healthily 'all the time'. I should be seeing more clients. I should be working more hours. I should spend more time being social. These and many other 'shoulds' were activities that I thought I could do if I had more energy.

But it suddenly occurred to me that even if I had more energy, these 'shoulds' weren't really relevant. What if I chose instead to do what I loved in a way that I loved. Instead of 'should', I 'could' do the things that I wanted to do.

I had to learn what was really important in my life and to let go of the rest. I had to relearn the way I did things, the way I started my day, and the way I engaged with life. All of this had to change in some way. I didn't know how I was going to do this, but I had to try. I had no other option. Either I continued a life of fatigue, distress, unfulfillment and compromise or I opened myself to the possibility that there was more out there for me. Life could be different. Health was still an option.

This proved to be the start of a long—at times tortuous—path into finding out who I was, reevaluating the choices I was making in my life, and how I could turn my health, fatigue, and direction in life into something joyous and positive. I had to learn who I was and how to become me.

I was finally coming out of hiding. I recognised that I was a people pleaser with a bright red flag hanging over my head! I finally admitted to myself who I was and had been for most of my life. It was time to change! It was time to let go of the 'good girl'. As my friend Karen Humphries said, 'I do not open the door to her anymore'. That little flame was starting to burn again. It was yearning for oxygen after having been extinguished for so long. I was ready to start a fire! Not just any fire but one huge glorious, vibrant, multi-coloured inferno.

So, I sat down and looked at what I needed to do. What could I hand over to others without too much guilt?

Why did I feel I had to be responsible for everything and everyone? Why in fact, do women generally feel responsible? Is it because of society's expectations of us or is it a cultural thing?

Most of us are brought up to be responsible for our actions. To admit when we are right or wrong and to be responsible citizens in our careers, our family life, and our interactions with others. This occurs for both men and women.

Why, however, do women generally feel 'more' responsible? Is it because we are the ones who bear children or usually act as carers and often take on more of the household duties?

I believe it is a combination of factors. Throughout history, women have taken on the roles of homemakers, child bearers and carers to their parents and families. Although women's roles in society have changed over the centuries, there is still a strong expectation for women to be responsible, look after their children, do many of the household chores, and to balance a career as well. Often these careers demand a high level of responsibility. My own early career as a nurse placed huge responsibilities on me, even when I was starting out as an eighteen-year-old.

How many women let go of these responsibilities and if they do, how many feel extremely guilty? I know I did. It took a lot of effort and courage for me to start asking for help. I know I needed it, but for someone who had always felt she was responsible for the whole world, this was a huge step. I started by asking for help around the house. First, I had to let go of controlling everything and accept that if I asked for help, things wouldn't be done in the same way. The house wouldn't be as clean and the meals would be different. Things wouldn't be done 'my way', but I had to be okay with that. My way wasn't working anymore.

This, however, took some negotiating.

After protesting that he was busy too, my husband agreed to take over the cooking one or two nights a week. Despite the complaints when it was his turn, he gradually adjusted and over time, he even took on the cooking a few more nights a week. When I threatened to hire a cleaner, he began to do most of the cleaning himself. Of course, there were arguments from him and criticism from me that things weren't done properly. 'You missed a bit. Look at that cobweb'. Yes, the house wasn't immaculate and he still couldn't stack the dishwasher properly, but did it really matter? I let go of the need to be perfect and the need to criticise, and I felt much better for it. I let go of some of that responsibility and a huge burden was lifted from my shoulders.

Though I rearranged the dishwasher at times and sometimes still do to this day! Like I said, no need to be perfect!

Ever so slowly, I realised how tightly I had held my life together and how fiercely I had fought for control over the things I had control over. Was it to protect me or the ones around me? Was it to keep myself safe or was it to help me feel better about myself so that I fit the role I had been assigned? The perfect wife and mother. Was it to validate my worth and contribution to my family and society? Was I doing all this for acceptance and recognition? Was this some hang up from childhood?

I decided to let it go and discover who I really was.

I began by reading some self-help books and one of the books that caught my eye was *You Can Heal Your Life* by Louise Hay[27].

This book literally changed my life. It's not some petty platitude. It really helped me redefine my life. Perhaps I was ready, perhaps the time was right. Perhaps it just crossed my path at the right time. Whatever the case, it was a life-changer for me.

Louise helped me realise just how little I really cared for and loved myself. Not just superficially but on a deeper level. I judged myself on my achievements, the perfect A's. The more courses I did, the higher grades I scored. The more I did for others, the better person I was. Or so I told myself. I had never thought about loving me, the person I was deep down when I was stripped of all my accomplishments and roles. The woman who had gifts and talents, sensitivity, and kindness without needing a piece of paper to prove it.

I had always liked myself but loved? Wasn't that something you did for others? What did it mean to love myself? I realised that I had no idea.

Louise has an exercise called 'mirror work', where you looked into the mirror each morning, looked into your eyes, and said 'I love you'. As I viewed the mirror every time I used the bathroom, I thought that this would be a simple, but probably ineffective, thing to do. I did it anyway. I mean, how hard could it be? The first time I did this, I thought it was silly and I laughed at myself. The next time I did it, I cried. I realised how little I really cared for myself and how little I really knew Judy. I had forgotten that little carefree girl who loved to dance and write and live through her vivid imagination.

I began to do things for myself. Slowly. Just because. And as I continued the 'mirror work' I noticed a softening in my features, a gentle warmth, and compassion for myself.

I learnt a new word. Self-care. What was it? Care of Self. It seems pretty obvious but how did I get started? What did it involve? Was it hard? Would it take more effort and energy?

It took time to adjust to this new way of thinking. It felt uncomfortable and unfamiliar. I slowly started to do things for myself.

When I went shopping, I bought myself flowers and had them gift-wrapped because I was worth it. I had always liked to dress well, but I took extra care with my clothes and makeup. I began to ask for help more. I was still trying to push through but not quite as vehemently, not quite as forcefully, as before. A gentler approach was more effective. I was starting to find me, though I still had a long way to go.

From caring comes courage.

LAO TZU

CHAPTER SIXTEEN
Caring

I first took on the role of a family carer soon after getting married. My mother had gone to visit her relatives in Hungary for the first time since she'd emigrated to Australia. My younger sister had travelled with her so my older sister and I took turns looking after Dad.

He came to stay with my husband and I in our rented home. He had signs of early dementia but he was otherwise okay. My mother had told me he was forgetful, but that was all. 'You just need to repeat instructions to him. He will be fine'.

This turned out to be the biggest understatement of all time!

I would leave him his lunch and go off to work, believing that all was fine. Each day when I returned, he seemed okay. Since he was out of his normal environment, I presumed it would take some time for him to adjust.

One day, however, I came home to the smell of something burning. The whole house smelled of smoke and ashes. I was terrified to see what I would find. Had something terrible happened to my father? I called out to Dad and he answered quietly so I knew at least that he was okay. I then entered the kitchen only to find the walls covered in soot and black smoke. "Oh my god! What happened?" I anxiously and rather angrily asked my father. He seemed oblivious to what was going on and shook his head. He seemed to have no understanding of what had happened and neither did I. I later found the plastic container with lunch didn't cope well on a gas flame!

My husband and I spent hours cleaning the kitchen walls while Dad looked on, seemingly unaware of the mess he had caused and the near disaster that he had avoided.

Dad's dementia was more severe than my sister and I had been led to believe and, suddenly, I became his carer. Attending to his hygiene, safety and meeting his needs was confronting. He wasn't showering properly or attending to his hygiene so the nurse in me stepped forwards and I took over. The daughter had to step aside. I felt sorry for him and I was angry at my mother for hiding the truth and putting me in this position. Why hadn't she told me what to expect?

Would I have still agreed to look after him? Yes, I probably would have. Would it have made a difference? Yes, definitely! I could have been better prepared.

My mother had a tendency to sweep things under the carpet. If something became too unpleasant, she would either defer dealing with it or pretend it hadn't happened. That was her way of coping. It served her and the roles she had taken on in her own life, perhaps due to the horrors of the war or as a way of dealing with life's difficulties. She appeared to have had a safe and idyllic upbringing. Perhaps the impact of the war and having to leave her birthplace so suddenly to escape the invading Russians, and having to start a whole new way of living, was too much to bear. I can only imagine how traumatic this must have been for her. The terror of being caught while escaping and the probable consequences would stay indelibly in her memory.

Trauma affects us in different ways and we all cope differently. What is right for one person may not serve another and most people don't know how they will deal with it. Recognising it is the first step and although Mum would speak of the events that affected her, I doubt she understood that they still had a lingering effect or perhaps she didn't want to discuss this.

Her behaviour, however, didn't serve me. I needed answers now rather than finding out the unpleasant truth by accident. When it was my sister's turn to look after Dad, he was more oriented back in his own environment. No disasters there.

While he was with me, I didn't question what I had to do, I just got on with it. He was my father and I was the 'good girl'. How could I step out of this role now, especially when he needed me? Once again, I slipped into my old patterns. After all I didn't know any better. Being there for others was what I did.

Until I finally stopped.

When my mother became elderly, I once again put things on hold. I saw no other way out and so I reverted to the old parts of me that stepped up when needed. This self-care thing wasn't easy. It needed constant attention and focus and as with any new habit, it could be easily derailed.

As my mother started to age, she developed early Alzheimer's, an awful disease that slowly took away the person I knew and loved. She was fortunate that it didn't affect her until later in life and that she only ever developed the early stages before her death. Over time, the family became used to the repetitive questions and the repetitive conversations we had with her as her short-term memory slowly drifted away. Some of her statements, however, became family mantras that we still use. Every time we drove to the countryside or the beach, she would say, 'It's so green'! During every meal she ate, she would say, 'This is the best chicken/meat that I have ever eaten'. She also lost her patience when waiting to be served in a restaurant and after waiting for a short period of time, she would loudly exclaim, 'Are they catching the chicken? They must be because it's taking so long.' Mum was quite deaf so her comments were widely heard! My darling mum was so loving and willing to please. Her words have become an inside joke that lovingly reminds us of her.

She slowly became more dependent on us, though she denied this and fiercely guarded her independence. She could manage at home alone. After all, she had had to for many years. But we started to notice little things that she no longer did. She had always been particular about hanging up her clothes, but I started to see outfits draped across her bed on a regular basis. Food was starting to deteriorate in the fridge, and she had stopped cleaning as thoroughly. She forgot conversations and instructions and so many of our chats became repetitive.

Despite her protests, and with much reluctance on her part, my sister and I arranged for carers to come in and do the cleaning for her and take her out shopping. I took her to various appointments, such as the local doctor, opticians, and the memory clinic, a total antithesis of what it represented. Patients didn't go there to find their memory but to realise how much of it they had actually lost. It was often a distressing hour or two for my mum and myself to experience.

My sister and I now had new roles. We were carers.

Like many women with older parents, our roles were suddenly reversed. Although Mum still cared for us all emotionally, she was unable to physically help out like she had throughout our lives. She had started to lose her perception and understanding. It was a huge adjustment for her to know that the role she had taken on so many years ago no longer had the same meaning.

To my sister and I, she was still our mother and she was still very dear to us, but a part of her had disappeared along with her memory and we grieved that loss. We could no longer go to her with our problems or get her advice on decisions. We would relate life occurrences and family events, but she had lost her perception and insight. While she could watch the news and tell you the day's happenings, she couldn't understand a difficulty I might have had or a dilemma I was dealing with. Our grieving took a long time and slowly we had to let her go. We were losing the mother she had once been and it was painful.

She was losing the person she had once been and although she didn't totally grasp this, she was also grieving how her life had changed.

The term carer can be such a misnomer. It means you provide care for those who need it, which is, in itself, a wonderful job. However, it doesn't take into account the lack of care you give yourself.

According to Australian statistics, 72% of primary carers are female[28]. Many communities and cultures see caring as a role for women. They expect women to take on these roles because it is often assumed that men have more important jobs to go to and women are better at caring! In my research, I discovered the term 'sandwich carers'. These are women who provide care to a child as well as an ageing parent.

Just like an actual sandwich, such women are squeezed between two inescapable situations. More responsibilities and less time for themselves. What if these women have careers as well as being carers? Are their needs even considered? No wonder anxiety, depression, and burnout occur. The twenty-first century saying, 'You can have it all', doesn't take into account the life of a carer! I also think this adage doesn't exist. Society paints a glamorous picture of manicured, immaculately groomed women juggling family and careers with ease.

This is far from reality with any woman, particularly if you are a carer. You attend to your parent's needs, scrape by with meeting the needs of your family and job, while having no room, energy, or inclination to attend to your own desires. Who said "You can have it all?"

Being a carer is exhausting. It can be fulfilling since you give back some of the love and attention your parents gave you, but it can also suck the life out of you. It often brings up guilt. Guilt that you are not doing enough for your parent, guilt that you are doing too much at the expense of your family, and guilt that you are neglecting yourself. No one wins.

As you try and navigate more demands on your time, you become more depleted. You rationalise that this isn't forever. You tell yourself that you will rest next week. But when next week comes, you tell yourself that next month is looking good.

How do we find a balance?

Balance means everything is in equal proportion and it's upright and steady. How could I find this under my current circumstances? I finally asked for help. When Mum started to have falls and could no longer cope at home, we hired an agency to find her suitable accommodation. I was good at guilt and the good girl had not gone away. She was ever present, particularly when a demanding situation arose.

I felt that I should bring Mum to live with me, but she adamantly refused. I felt guilty because she said no, and I felt guilty because

I was relieved that she had. Asking her appeased my guilt to some extent, but a part of me felt I could have tried harder. Was I willing to give up my life to be a full-time carer? I didn't think I could. Also, what about my family? Was it fair to them? More guilt. More indecision. Not knowing which way to go. The answers are never right or wrong and whatever conclusion you come to, you're never truly satisfied.

I also learned not to give up on my need to change the new way I was living. Yes, I wanted to be there for my mother, but I also knew that I needed to be there for myself. I studied mediation more deeply and I began a daily practice. I found it incredibly hard to sit still for twenty to thirty minutes so I rationalised that five minutes was better than nothing. I didn't have any more time! I soon found that while five minutes was a great starting point, I really needed to do more to relax and I could make time.

I started to get up half an hour earlier on work days and gradually increased my meditation time. I realised that despite the mindless chatter that still went on in my head, I was starting each day more relaxed and in a better frame of mind. This meditation thing was my new friend with benefits!

As my mother continued to deteriorate, my sister and I found her accommodations at an aged care facility. There was an enormous amount of guilt around placing her there, but we knew we couldn't cope and that she would receive the care that she needed. Once she was settled, I stepped back a little. I still visited her regularly because I wanted to, but I let go (a little) of the obligation to be the perfect daughter. I knew she was being well cared for and I also realised that I needed time for myself, even if it wasn't every day. I still managed her finances and paid her bills, but the need to be physically present had somewhat eased.

That long-held tension was slowly easing. I was allowing myself to breathe again.

Real freedom is saying 'no' without giving a reason.

AMIT KALANTRI

CHAPTER SEVENTEEN
No Is An Actual Word

Although I grieved her loss when my mother passed away, I suddenly found I had more time. I was tempted to work longer hours, as the 'good girl' hadn't yet gone away, but I was still really fatigued. My 'shoulds' were still ever present.

I have more time, so I should help more at home again. I should take over all the cooking. I should see my friends more. I should volunteer for my reflexology association. I should see more clients. I should take over the cleaning once again.

The pressure to be available to others and help out was still present. Why do we do this? Why do women feel they have to give so much of themselves? Is it because society sees us as the carers, the givers, the ones who have time? Or is it our own beliefs and experiences that perpetuate this behaviour? Perhaps it's a bit of both.

We don't always take on these roles consciously. Due to our upbringing and societal expectations, many women assume that they will care for their ageing parents. After all, it is mainly women who raise and care for their children. We run our households, have careers, care for our partners, parents, and pets. We rarely question these roles. Although this is changing, many men still tend to be on the periphery. It's us brave, courageous, unselfish women who put ourselves forward. Why shouldn't we?

Who are we kidding? As women, I believe we prostitute ourselves. We sell ourselves to those who are the most persuasive, the most forceful, the most emotional, or the most needy. We often settle for lesser jobs, get paid pittance, accept the breadcrumbs.

Actually, we don't even sell ourselves. We just give ourselves away. We feel that we should help others. We can't ignore their pleas. Others need us now. Others are more deserving. Other's needs are greater.

We tell ourselves so many stories that we soon start to believe the lies.

Why do we feel that we need to serve the needs of others before we meet our own needs? Is it a gender or generational issue or due to society's expectations of us as women and what's considered the norm? Is it a sign of perfectionism yet again? The need to be doing the right thing, whatever that is. The need to be accepted and loved. Perhaps that's all it comes down to.

Why do we hurt ourselves? We may not stick pins into ourselves, but we hurt ourselves in many other ways. We neglect our bodies, we don't exercise, we drink too much, we eat the wrong foods, we think ill of ourselves, we don't rest, and we keep pushing through. We don't ask for help when we really need it and we're afraid to show others how we're feeling. We still believe we need to do it all.

Why do we feel we have to prove ourselves and to whom?

A counsellor once said to me that the word 'should' needs to be removed from the English language. 'Should' implies that you must acquiesce to someone else's needs regardless of your own needs or your time, your energy, or desires. 'Should' implies you don't have needs or desires yourself and that others always deserve attention first.

How do we treat a child? Usually with unconditional love and tenderness. Why can't we do this for ourselves? Why can't we love ourselves instead?

Chapter Seventeen » No Is An Actual Word

I learnt another new word. It was No!

I finally realised that I needed to put my needs first. That was probably pretty obvious to many, but for a lifelong perfectionist and people pleaser like me, it wasn't blatantly so. It's such a simple word but it carries so many burdens.

'No' brings up guilt and obligation. It dashes hopes and dreams. It dismisses questions and curiosities. It ends conversations and it brings up discomfort and vulnerabilities. It leaves you open to be judged and criticised. It feels so final with no going back. It feels selfish and irresponsible. It brings up feelings of unworthiness.

Who am I to refuse you or your request or your needs?

'No', however, is one of the most important words we will ever learn. It is also one of the hardest to say.

Most of us want to be liked. We care what others think of us. We worry about how others will view us and we crave acceptance. We feel that if we turn down opportunities, jobs, invitations, or requests from others, we will be judged or, even worse, rejected. We avoid being the one left behind, the difficult one, the one who always questions everything, the one who needs to know why. And so, we give in.

Often, we are unaware of the patterns we are constantly repeating, but even when awareness kicks in, we still resist. It's far easier to say 'Yes.' We tell ourselves we can defer what we're doing, rest later, make up for it another day when someone really needs our help. We can say 'No' next time. But we're only lying to ourselves and selling ourselves short. We are, once again, not meeting our own needs.

We end up depleted, resentful, exhausted, and often ill.

I, too, have said no to friends, only to feel extreme guilt afterwards. I have dinner a few times a year with a group of old nursing friends and usually don't know if I will feel up to it by the time the arranged date arrives.

I always accept these invitations in good faith, but I often have to excuse myself because of extreme fatigue. I have always made up some excuse, such as 'I have a cold', but I always feel guilty afterwards. I don't tell them that I'm too tired since I feel that they wouldn't understand. I fear being judged or criticised.

Gabor Mate says that when we don't express our own needs and feelings effectively, our physiology is also affected. Chronic emotional stress affects our immune system. When our needs aren't met in childhood, we play out our behaviours as adults. We compensate for the things we missed out on or the behaviours that affected our upbringing. We over-parent or over-mother or over-care for everyone else but overlook ourselves. He says, "When we have been prevented from learning how to say no, our bodies may end up saying it for us."[29]

Constantly living in a state of anxiety and fear will only lead to disease. As Franklin D. Roosevelt said in his inaugural speech, "The only thing we have to fear....is fear, itself."[30]

Constant stress leads to an elevation of our stress hormones and has been linked to most major illnesses.[31]

Denying our own needs leads to a life of drudgery and we lose our joy and excitement in living. Life becomes a burden instead of the magical, wonderful, and joyous adventure it really is.

I started to look for more answers and I finally learned about boundaries.

A boundary is a defining or limiting line that clearly separates or protects a person or property from another. It's like the fences or walls we have between our homes to separate us from our neighbours. We have them for privacy and to claim ownership over our territory.

We may keep a distance from strangers or people we don't know to protect ourselves. We don't hang around in dark laneways at night (hopefully) or go to dodgy areas by ourselves. We have boundaries around these things so that we are protected and kept safe. When we speak to someone we don't know very well, we keep a slight distance from them. We do this to protect our personal space, our boundary around what feels comfortable to us. But when it comes to how we speak, treat ourselves, or allow others to treat us, things are not so obvious.

Personal boundaries are values that we have learnt or adhered to throughout our lives. They define what is acceptable behaviour and what isn't and determine what areas we take responsibility for. We learn these in childhood and adjust what feels comfortable to us as we mature and grow. They are often not clear cut and sometimes become muddled as they usually involve an emotional response. However for us to lead happy and fulfilled lives, boundaries are essential[32].

Boundaries are about how we treat ourselves and how we allow others to treat us. They are physical, emotional, or mental limits that we place around ourselves for protection and as part of our self-worth.

I realised that my personal boundaries were weak and in disrepair. Had they ever existed or had I slowly let them erode? Obviously, I had learnt what was acceptable behaviour in social situations and amongst society, but what about the boundaries I put up around myself? I began to look at all the ways mine were missing or needed renovation, and there were many.

As a lifelong people pleaser, I had been giving away all of myself. I suddenly realised that the more you give and give of yourself, the more you deplete your energy and joy and the less there will be for you. Trust me! I did this for so many years only to finally realise that my life, my happiness, and my fulfilment must come from filling my cup first.

Not negotiable!

Of course, this doesn't happen overnight and changes can be slow. After a lifetime of perfecting the 'people pleaser', don't expect things to change overnight. It takes time and awareness and, mostly, it takes compassion, especially when you get it wrong and fall back into old behaviours.

I ran a home-based business, but I would allow clients to ring me at all hours and even on weekends. Although I had an answering machine and voice messaging, I still picked up the phone. I always ran over time with clients because I felt that I could give them extra treatment that they would benefit from. The good girl was raising her hand again. However, I gradually realised that I wasn't respecting my time or theirs.

I started to set strict time limits on when I was available and kept my appointments (mainly) to their allocated times. I didn't always get it right, but I became better at it with practice. When I was asked to help out with something, instead of feeling pressured to say yes, which I had always done, I would say, 'Can I get back to you?' This gave me some breathing space. This also meant that I didn't commit myself and gave myself time to decide if I really wanted to commit or if the request actually suited me or my available energy. I also found that if I didn't maintain my boundaries, I would become resentful. I felt that others were taking advantage of me, but really, I was the one who was allowing this behaviour to happen.

I began to realise that having boundaries around what I did was a part of loving myself. Setting limits on my availability wasn't that comfortable since I wanted to be liked and well thought of. However, if I was only saying yes to keep the peace or make someone else happy, I was ultimately selling myself short and disappointing myself.

Self-love means that you are respecting all of you — the way you look, the way you dress, the actions you take, and the decisions you make. It meant that I got to decide what was okay and what wasn't acceptable to me.

Do you have friends that are always late whenever you meet up?

This may not be intentional, but it shows a lack of respect towards themselves and is disrespectful to you. If you begin to respect your own boundaries around time, they may learn to do the same. Many people don't even realise they are doing this.

I have mentioned this to clients who are always late. Most of the time they don't even realise their behaviour. When we discuss this, they start to realise how their actions are playing out throughout their lives. They may feel they need to fit in 'just one more thing.' They feel they are trying not to disappoint others. They realise they are placing huge expectations on themselves.

It's usually not black and white. They are rarely just late. There is often something underlying at play. Sometimes it's a learned behaviour or a belief from childhood. Sometimes it's a lack of self-worth or value.

Do you have friends that chat for hours on the phone? I do and I would often find this exhausting. Now if I'm getting tired, I gently cut the conversation short. I tell them that I have things to do. I don't need to justify my actions.

When you begin to set limits on your time, not everyone will be happy. They have become used to the old 'available' you. They may have their own beliefs around availability and obligation. That's okay. You can explain what you are doing or not. Just be firm with your decisions. They may not please everyone, but that's not why you're here!

How do others treat you at work? How do you allow them to? Are you always taking on extra tasks that could be performed by someone else? Are you always staying late to meet the demands of someone else?

Sometimes this is inevitable as we may have deadlines to meet or choose to stay back and complete some more work. But if this is you and you are doing it all the time, then take a look at your boundaries and ask yourself if you could just for once say no.

By saying no when we want to, we maintain our own positive self-worth. We maintain integrity and honesty in our relationships and have a say in how we live our lives. When we draw a line in the sand, we are establishing our sense of identity, who we are, and what is important to us. We learn to not rely on others for our self-worth. We give ourselves permission to be us. Who we really are.

In turn, we learn to recognise our own needs and stop putting ourselves last, something that I believe most women do on a regular basis. This was my story too. I believed that everyone else's needs were more important than my own.

However, over time, I learned to accept more help and ask for it. I rested when I needed to, even if it was just sitting with my eyes closed for ten minutes. I began to have an earlier bedtime and slept in when I didn't have appointments. I finally learned to be gentle with myself. I recognised that if I wasn't there for me first, I could never be there for anyone else. By putting boundaries in place, I learnt to allow my own individuality to come through and in doing so, I learnt to respect and recognise the individuality of others.

Then just when you think you have it all sorted, your boundary is once more threatened like some insidious beast. It creeps up on you when least expected and strikes unwittingly. You are once more its victim.

I was, by now, pretty in touch with my needs and boundaries. I knew, more or less, when I needed to say no, when my body needed rest, and when I needed some 'alone' time. However, a phone call from a close friend changed all of that. We chatted happily for a few minutes. Then, I asked her to share her week. Two hours later, we said goodbye and then, exhausted, I hit a brick wall.

I started to berate myself. Why had I talked for so long? Why hadn't I cut the conversation short? Why had I put myself into this situation once again? Wasn't I in charge of my boundaries? Why had I stuffed up yet again?

Then I finally realised that this boundary thing was ongoing. I didn't need to criticise myself or be angry about my actions. It was a learning curve. I was still learning and, perhaps, I always would be. So much of our behaviour is learned in childhood. If our needs are ignored, we feel we need to justify ourselves as adults. If we are only validated for the things we achieve, we will always strive for perfectionism. If we are scared to speak up as children, we stay small and silent as adults.

We create patterns in our behaviour and keep repeating them until we learn otherwise. Even when we learn awareness, it is still very easy to fall back into old patterns. Our egos are powerful dictators.

Self-care doesn't always come naturally. If we haven't received care and nurturing as a child, it is difficult to give it to ourselves as adults. Once learned, it is an ongoing business. It takes effort, it takes time, and most of all, it takes awareness. It also takes courage. Courage to be yourself and put yourself first.

The more you practice it, the more accomplished you become. I will probably stuff up again, but I know that it's okay. Each time I do, I will become even more aware and one day I'll learn to automatically put myself first.

That's what I'm planning anyway.

The important thing
is not to stop questioning.
Curiosity has its own reason
for existing.

ALBERT EINSTEIN

CHAPTER EIGHTEEN
What's On The Other Side?

Have you given up everything for your profession? At what cost? Has it been overwhelming for you? Have you lost your soul, given up all your hopes and dreams of being someone or something that you are no longer sure you want to be, in the pursuit of a particular role?

Have you considered the roles we assign to others? Why do we put people on a pedestal? Sports stars, movie stars and rockstars are often considered to be higher gods. We see them as heroes who can do no wrong. Do we expect too much of them? They are after all just human beings. They think, feel, love, and exist the same as we do. Yes, they may have hugely extravagant lives, but they feel the same emotions and thoughts that all humans do.

We, however, see them as superhuman beings. We elevate them to unrealistic heights and when they fall, which they inevitably do because they have all the same human frailties, we destroy and abandon them.

How do you talk about yourself? Do your words define you?

We are daughters, sisters, wives, partners, friends, mothers. We have careers and jobs. We also have dreams. We are much more than the roles we take on in life. Yet so few of us explore what we are really capable of.

I, myself, have so many dreams, so many tasks that I want to undertake, and so many things that I want to achieve. I get excited and start a new project, a bold and exciting project but often don't follow through. Have you done this too? Why?

Is it because you realise it's not as bold and exciting as you thought after all, or is it because it's too bold and exciting?

Does fear hold you back? Is it safer to play small?

Is it safer to not speak up, speak out, or speak about yourself?

What if you did?

What if you took action?

What if you actually engaged?

What if you realised that your role—or roles—in life were limiting?

What would happen?

Would you be criticised or, even worse, judged?

What if you were to become successful, or famous, or wealthy?

Would that frighten you?

Would you be overwhelmed? Would your friends and family still treat you the same, or would they abandon you?

Isn't it safer, then, to stay small, stay hidden, cocooned in your own home in your status quo and not cause too many waves?

"Yes, it is," a small voice inside you says. 'But then I would never know what I'm capable of achieving! I would never know what great things I could create. I would never know the fun I could have or what a fulfilled life really is'.

Garrett Gravesen speaks about taking 10 seconds of insane courage[33]. When we want to try something new or something really scary, every part of us screams not to do it. Our minds envisage the worst possible outcome. We fear failure. We feel we will be doomed. That's exactly when we need to find ten seconds of insane courage and take action.

When my mother was very old and in a nursing home, I bought her a beautiful rose bush. It was a deep velvety red with the most divine fragrance. She loved it. We placed it outside her room so that she could see it whenever she looked out the windows. She then said these words to me, 'I wish I could paint that rose'.

When she was a child, she had once been praised for a painting she did. She'd described how proud she felt to receive such praise. She had never pursued a career in the arts as she didn't believe she had any talents in that field. When she said these words to me, I replied softly, 'It's never too late. I'll bring you some paints and you can try'.

But she never did.

Don't get to old age only to wish that you had tried. Don't regret not giving it a go. Paint that rose, climb that mountain, take that photo, write that book, dance to the music, and sing that song.

If we never try to fly, we might one day die, always wondering what if. Don't let that be your life! As Garrett says, "Let go. Life happens outside your comfort zone."[34] We need to experience those things that often terrify us. We need to step out of our safe and limiting havens.

When I was a child, my mother would take us on long walks on the beach or along mountain trails. She was always curious and full of life. When we were tired and ready to go home, she would say, 'Let's just see what's on the other side.' She always wanted to know what was around the next corner, over the next hill, or around the next bay.

Sometimes it was more of the same. The same corner, the same mountain or same seaside cove. But every so often it was a new discovery, a wonder to behold, a sight so amazing that we could easily have missed it, if we hadn't gone to see what was on the other side.

Always keep that sense of wonder and curiosity about you. If you're not sure how to do this, just say to yourself, 'Let's see what's on the other side.'

The best and most beautiful
things in the world cannot
be seen or even touched.
They must be felt with the heart.

HELEN KELLER

CHAPTER NINETEEN
Emotions

In my journey to find myself and what roles and behaviours I could let go of, I knew that I needed to look at all of me—my sense of self, sensitivity, and worth. How had these influenced the woman I had become and how could I change my perception around them? I began by looking at my emotions, a part of me that had always governed my actions and decisions.

What role do emotions play in our lives? Are they that significant or do they get in the way? Do our emotions help or hinder us? What role do they play in our life and how much influence do they have on the lives we live?

Do they even matter?

Our emotions are our feelings, the ways we see ourselves and others, and how we interact with the world. They are our happy, laughing, angry, sad, tearful, and joyous feelings that show we are alive and human. If we didn't show our emotions, we would appear robotic, unfeeling, and uncaring.

I had always seen myself as emotional as I cried easily, felt things deeply and was labelled 'sensitive.' It was seen as a failing, a curse, and not something to be proud of.

Consequently, many of us hide our emotions. We are too scared to show others what we are really feeling. We fear being judged. Think of a child that throws a tantrum in the supermarket. Most people look judgmentally at the mother. Why can't she control her child? Why isn't he or she well behaved? Why is the child being so naughty?

Society doesn't encourage us to show our feelings. If we laugh too loudly, talk too much, or show too much anger or even too much joy, we are judged. It feels far safer to be quiet, to blend in with the crowd, to appear as everyone else. And that's in public.

What about our private selves? Do we still keep our deepest feelings hidden? Were we encouraged to behave as children to be good and obedient? I know that I certainly was. I wasn't allowed to be angry or yell too much. I was brought up to be a lady, whatever that meant. I guess it meant that I suppressed my feelings and reactions. I remained quiet and in the background. I pushed down my rage and I suppressed my fears. I avoided confrontation as it felt too stressful.

Don't get me wrong. I enjoyed life. I laughed a lot and loved and cried, but that was within limits. To my family, I was quiet and well behaved. With my close friends, I could be more myself. I could share more of my feelings and thoughts and fears, but I still presented a veneer to the world. I showed up as I expected others would see me. I thought society expected this of me. I was terrified of showing who the real me was. What if I let everyone down and they thought I was too quiet, boring or, even worse, disappointing?

How many of us live within the boundaries that society has placed on us and, as a result, placed on ourselves? How many of us are too scared of being rejected or judged or thought to be different? And what if we were different? Wouldn't this be a healthier and happier version of ourselves?

Isn't it more beneficial to show our emotions?

In her book, *Molecules of Emotion*, neuroscientist Candace Pert, Ph.D.[35] talks about the connection between our emotions and our minds and how blocked emotions lead to disease. She discusses how chemicals are released in response to different emotions. When blocked emotions are released through touch or other methods, the energy pathways in our body are restored.

A child who throws a tantrum may not be misbehaving but rather expressing their fear or insecurity. If a child isn't allowed to express how they are feeling, they may show their feelings in ways that as adults, we find unacceptable. A child is too immature to understand their feelings or talk about them so they demonstrate them in often unsettling ways. How we, as adults, react to their behaviour will determine their future reactions.

Dr Mona Delahooke, Ph.D.[36] says that such misbehaviour is often a body's response to stress. If a child is stressed but doesn't understand or can't explain how she or he is feeling, they will act out and misbehave. It's often the only way they can express their fears. It isn't necessarily wilful or intentional.

As adults, we have learnt not to do this. We have learnt that we can't throw a tantrum in a supermarket, no matter how much we might want to. We repress our feelings until a more socially acceptable time and even then, we often bury them.

I rarely showed anger. If something upset me, I buried my feelings or ran away from the situation. I hated confrontation. In a childhood where it was safer to not answer back or question my father, I learnt to not show my rage. My father did enough of that so I learnt to repress mine.

It was only as an adult, and many years into my marriage, that I faced my truths. It was okay to be angry and face the situation. I didn't need to change the subject, something that I was an expert at. Does this sound familiar? So many of us opt out when a conversation or situation becomes uncomfortable.

I realised that it was safe to have differences and heated discussions. It was okay to feel passionate about a topic and it was safe to express my views.

So many of us keep quiet in case we rock the boat. If someone disagrees with us, we feel criticised. However, it's important to remember that if someone has a different opinion or becomes angry, it isn't always about us. Their beliefs and experiences had shaped them and the roles that they had taken on in life. They are reacting as a result of their own upbringing and learned patterns. My own experiences had shaped me and who I had become. I was responsible for my reactions and behaviour but definitely not for theirs.

It was safe to show myself and all of who I was. I didn't need to compare myself to others. I didn't need to conform. I could be me in all my glory, magnificence, messiness, and humanness. I was learning to stand up for myself and share my opinions and thoughts.

My sensitivity was a gift. I was starting to recognise myself and my self-worth.

I was finally discovering my voice.

You are uniquely and originally you. Be bold and daring and fearless and unconventional. Be willing to use your voice in service to your soul. Go on. Rock that damn boat. The wave you create might just change the world.

CHERYL RICHARDSON

CHAPTER TWENTY
Rock The Boat

When I started my reflexology business, I thought it had to be run in a certain way. I listened to my peers and various mentors and enjoyed some success. I charged what others were charging and worked all hours under the sun. I followed the advice of coaches and then wondered why I still wasn't satisfied and why I was so tired and burnt out. They were making money. They were successful and healthy. Why wasn't I?

I realised that there was nothing wrong with following their guidance, but I wasn't listening to my own inner compass. The part of me that always guides me home. The part of me that speaks my truth.

I was also playing it safe. How many of us do that? How many of us stay in the same jobs, the same marriages, the same friendships, even when they no longer make us happy? We do it because if feels comfortable and it feels safe. Change is scary and unpredictable. It opens us up to vulnerability and to criticism. It opens us up to making mistakes and we risk failure. I was the same.

Each month, I would send out newsletters to my mailing list. Initially I did a lot of research for these articles and spoke about the benefits of reflexology for their health.

Every so often I would write about boundaries and topics that could benefit them emotionally.

However, I always toed the line. I wrote safe articles, ones that weren't too controversial. I didn't want to rock the boat or create too much disharmony. I was also scared of people unsubscribing. Over time, I realised that I wasn't totally being me. I wasn't sharing my true voice. I was playing it safe yet again.

If I really wanted to use my voice as a powerful vehicle, I needed to share more of me. So, slowly, I spoke about my feelings and incidents in my life. The ones that had helped me grow the most. The ones that had affected me deeply.

I pressed send and then waited to see how many would unsubscribe. The odd one did, but generally most didn't and many even emailed me back to say how much my stories had resonated with them. The more authentic I was, the more connected I was with my list.

I began to write more freely and shared my thoughts and values. I didn't expect everyone to agree, but I wanted to inspire others to take action and change their lives. To be motivated to know that change was possible if they wanted it badly enough.

How can you find your voice when it's been hidden for so long? How can it feel safe to do so when in the past, it wasn't? Will there be repercussions if you do? Will you be judged? Will you be punished like you were as a child?

It's very easy to convince yourself that you should keep your opinions to yourself.

Perhaps share them with your family or close friends but don't speak up. It's much safer that way. When so much attention is centred on social media, any wrong or misjudged comment will have repercussions.

However, if you continue to live your life playing it safe, you'll never experience life in all its glory. Life isn't meant to be played safe. It's meant to be lived loudly, vibrantly, and messily.

I considered all these things as I began to spend more time on social media. At first, I used it to promote my business but began to see it as a platform for speaking my truth. I was terrified of so-called trolls or haters who would judge me and, at first, I deleted controversial posts. I avoided discussing politics or current affairs that drew condemnation. I contributed to pleasant chatter. I played it safe.

But I gradually realised that no matter what I wrote, not everyone was going to like it. Not everyone would be delighted. I have friends who would never discuss their private lives or childhoods in detail and would criticise me or judge me for doing this very thing. It's not a comfortable feeling to know that I might be criticised. I know that not everyone will like my writing, or a piece of poetry, or a photograph that I might share. Not everyone will be interested in my latest news or tips. That's okay. I decided that so long as I was kind and civil, I could express my views.

Remember everyone isn't going to be satisfied with what you do or say. We are all different human beings with different likes and dislikes. We come from an enormous variety of backgrounds with an enormous variety of experiences. We won't all like the same things. It's okay to be different or else the world would be an extremely boring place.

So, I decided to change the way I ran my business. I worked days and times that suited me. I charged prices that I felt reflected the value of my services and I ignored what others were doing and charging. It worked and I attracted clients who resonated with my authenticity and expertise.

We are not here to please everybody. In fact, that's impossible. There will always be someone who disagrees with your point of view, or the clothes you wear, or the way you live your life.

Living our lives authentically is the only way to live. If we need to step out of our current circumstances to find happiness and self-worth, then it's vital we listen to that inner voice. If we need to let go of the roles we have taken on throughout our lives, then it's important to follow that nudge or instinct.

If we are accepted by others, that's great. If not, that's okay too. It's more important to accept ourselves and keep on rocking that boat.

Abandon the idea that you will forever be the victim of the things that have happened to you. Choose to be a victor.

SETH ADAM SMITH

CHAPTER TWENTY-ONE
Playing The Victim

If you are diagnosed with an illness, or experience some major change or trauma, this can change your life and how you see yourself. Whether it be chronic fatigue, as in my case, or cancer, rheumatoid arthritis, fibromyalgia, multiple sclerosis, or any other chronic condition or a traumatic event, changes have to be made to your life.

You may have to slow down and work part-time or you may not be able to work at all for a time. You may have to renavigate how you work, socialise, play, and generally go about your life. Often, these changes are temporary until your physical or mental health improves or they may require a new permanent change.

Where do you fit in? Who are you? Are you still the same person or has your role in life now changed?

A chronic condition may cause pain, a decrease in movement, fatigue, digestive issues, anxiety, irritability, and frustration. There is also the shock and emotional trauma of a diagnosis to deal with. What can you do to make life better? How do you deal with something that you may have to live with for many years?

Change isn't necessarily bad. It may open up a new way of living for us. Sometimes, it's a much healthier and more fulfilling way.

However, it's easy to get caught up in the diagnosis or circumstance and suddenly see your role as life-changing. Maybe you were the main breadwinner, the main carer, the happy and capable one, but suddenly your life is turned upside down. Maybe you were the social, outgoing life of the party who can no longer stay up past 9pm or feel uncomfortable going out on your own. Maybe you were the adventurous one who climbed mountains and now can barely walk down your street.

You have to make allowances for your fatigue, pain, and your treatments and then alter how you live your life. Your illness can feel all-encompassing. It's very easy to see yourself as a victim and ask, 'Why me?' It's very easy to feel powerless. There may be times where you feel despondent or fed up. There may be times where you rebel, feel angry, or just give up.

Victimhood is an easy mantle to wear.

I know because I've been there. I see many clients in my reflexology clinic with an assortment of ailments. Some were more serious than others. However, I always encouraged my clients not to see themselves as victims.

I suddenly realised that I was beginning to see myself as one, as someone who was wounded, not whole, especially when I was feeling at my lowest. It's amazing how easy it is to do this. As the morning light enters your bedroom and you wake up after another long night, you realise that you still aren't feeling well. The anonymity of sleep allows you to forget your ailments and situation, even if it's only for a few hours. However, the cold reality of the day quickly reminds you and it becomes very easy to shift your focus onto how you're feeling once more. You begin to see life through these tinted glasses that place everything around you within that bubble of your diagnosis.

The same can happen if you experience a trauma or when you lose someone close to you. Others feel sorry for you and you become immersed in the circumstances of your life.

At first, I didn't question my thoughts or my behaviour. It was just how it was. I became caught up in my symptoms when I wasn't feeling well. Everything in my life began to centre around me. I didn't realise what I was doing. I was so caught up in myself that all my decisions came from a place of coping or not.

I started to question my self-worth. If I couldn't be who I was before, or do the things I had done before, what was my role in life? Who would I be? What could I do?

If you aren't feeling well, or are severely stressed, your tolerance for coping diminishes and you do whatever you can to avoid overwhelm. You may cut down the hours you work. You learn to say no to many social engagements. You start to ask for help, much more than you want to. You feel very much a victim of your circumstances and you start to feel that you have no control. Life is happening to you. You also feel guilty. Guilty for asking for help, guilty for feeling you are letting others down, guilty for saying no once again.

Life becomes a one-day-at-a-time occasion. You become frightened and anxious about planning too far ahead. Like so many other women who wear an assortment of hats, I didn't know how to juggle the roles I had taken on in life. When you are still trying to figure out who you are and how you fit in, any deviation, such as an illness or trauma, can totally throw you off kilter.

Playing the victim isn't healthy but it's so easy to fall into this mode of thinking. Your life has changed for whatever reason. Your circumstances now dictate how each day unfolds. You believe you are no longer the same person. You can't do the same things you did before or live the life you once had. Or so it seems.

I began to realise that focusing solely on my symptoms wasn't helping me. I was only feeling sorry for myself. There was still so much I could do with my life and perhaps reassessing how I had reached this point, might help. I could take back control!

I started to look back at my life and the patterns that possibly led to my initial fatigue. Playing the good girl, being the perfectionist, and saying yes to everyone eventually led to burnout. As to being chronically fatigued, I don't have the answers. There are many reasons for it occurring and many of them are unknown[37]. It has been linked to a past infection, excessive stress, mould, tick infections, an immune imbalance, and a myriad other reasons.

The reasons why don't really matter to me. It happened and I needed to learn how to deal with it. My illness didn't need to be my life story. I had choices.

I learned to change my perspective.

In photography, when I go to capture a view or image, I choose a certain outlook. I take a few photos then I change the view. It may be slightly off centre or taken from a different angle. I may kneel or even lie down. This simple action changes the whole image.

In business, I found that I can alter my messaging and how I choose to engage with clients. I can choose to do things my way, not necessarily the way others are running their businesses. I can change my perspective and how I view the world.

The same can be said about health. When I needed to have lots of blood tests, procedures, and medication to resolve a health issue, I saw these as setbacks that were preventing me from moving forwards. They were annoyances and just another thing to get through. They were getting in the way of my life.

Then I realised that all of these actions were actually helping me to move forwards towards great health, not away from it. The tests were necessary to find a diagnosis and a treatment.

I changed my perspective.

Whatever you do, you have a choice in how you view life and how events and circumstances will affect you. You can always choose to change your perspective and your point of view. Yes, crappy things happen. Our circumstances may change and not always for the better. Our emotional and financial state and our health may be altered, but we can choose how we view such things and how we react to them.

We can also choose to change our perception. Our perception is based on our senses, how we see, hear, or interpret something. It is based on our beliefs, experiences, and values. Perspective is how we look at life and perception is how we choose to experience it. One influences the other.

Scientist and cell biologist, Dr Bruce Lipton found that by changing our perception[38], we are directly influencing the chemistry of our body. Think of the placebo effect. If someone is given a medicine that they believe will make them better, it will, even if it's just a sugar pill.

Such is the power of our mind over our body. Dr Lipton showed that changing our perception actually changes the chemistry inside our body.

Just think of how powerful this can be, both on an emotional and physical level.

If we change our views on our illnesses or our life's circumstances and then, how we choose to experience them, we can make profound changes in our overall health and well-being. If we change our view on our current situation, we can change how we react to it.

Another realisation I came to was that my illness doesn't define me. It is not who I am!

It is something that I have to deal with, but it's just a label. I didn't need to be a victim.

Each one of us is an individual with a unique personality. We may love nature, dancing, the gym, reading, meditation, travelling or a million other things.

We may be gentle, serious, creative, studious, or wacky souls. If we have an illness or a major upheaval, it is a part of our lives, certainly for the present. We may have to alter the way we work or participate in activities, but that doesn't mean our lives our less meaningful.

It does not make a victim out of us. This realisation helped me to understand that there was so much more to my life. I had taken on many roles—some out of obligation, some out of necessity, some out of fear or anxiety—but playing the victim was not one of them.

I needed to reassess my worth and sense of self. I was ready to move on.

When you lose all sense
of self the bonds of
a thousand chains will vanish.
Lose yourself completely,
return to the root of
the root of your own soul.

RUMI

CHAPTER TWENTY-TWO

Worth

If you read any self-help book, magazine, or social media post, there is so much talk about worth. You are worthy. What, then, is worth and how do you measure it? Why does it matter?

Just think of a handbag that you bought for a certain price. It may hold far more value than its monetary cost. It may have been a gift from a friend or hold special memories of an event where you wore it on your shoulder, in that perfect dress in that little café in Paris. You may just love its shape, or that gorgeous colour, or maybe it's just the right size to hold all your personal stuff.

Worth carries emotion with it so it's never easy to judge. It holds memories of special times and places or people who touched your life. It's hard enough when you attach worth to an object you own or wear, but how do you measure your own worth?

As a child, I learned to value myself according to my achievements. The higher grades I received, the more worthy I was. Perfectionism became my mantra and I pushed and pushed myself to do better, try harder, do more courses, and gain more knowledge so that I was worthy. I never questioned why. It was just the way life was. If I could become the best version of me, I must surely be worthy. What was I trying to prove? That I was worthy of love, of belonging, of acceptance? That I had value?

So many of us attach a meaning to worth. We believe that we need to do something to be worthy. We need to prove to others that we hold value. That we deserve their attention and love. We can't just be ourselves. It isn't enough. Society encourages this and measures our success by our achievements. We need to show something for our efforts or be someone to earn recognition and acceptance.

My father expected a lot from his daughters. He worked hard, paid for our education, and expected us to study and achieve great grades. We weren't encouraged to lie around reading romance novels. In fact, this was frowned upon. We had to be productive. Yes, there was a time for play, but work and study took priority. I guess his own upbringing had instilled these beliefs in him. As an only child of a divorced mother, he worked and studied hard himself. He saw how hard his own mother worked. Maybe he felt he had to prove himself to her. As an immigrant in a new country, these traits had helped him get a steady job, a wife, and a family. We were loved, but we all had to navigate our way into loving ourselves.

As an adult, I continued to try and prove myself, especially in my work. As a nurse I felt I had to prove to everyone that I was responsible. Because I showed I was competent, I was often put in charge of busy wards. Then I would put extra pressure on myself to demonstrate that I was in fact responsible and nothing went wrong, so that the faith put in me was justified. How crazy was that? Despite that, I continued to doubt myself and my capabilities.

How many of us still do this?

Why do we feel that our peers and employers will accept us more and regard us more highly if we stay late, put in more hours, and 'prove' that we are worthy? We aim for perfectionism and set higher and higher, often unachievable standards for ourselves.

Perhaps this reflects society's values based on material success. The harder we work, the more we can earn. The more we earn, the higher our self-worth. Is this sustainable? I don't think so.

I believe that there comes a time when our happiness has to take priority. We put off so much of our lives, put off truly living, in the pursuit of more money, more products, more work, more 'I'll just do this before…'

Before I rest.

Before I have a holiday.

Before I have fun.

Before I find what really makes me happy.

Before it is/I am perfect.

I'm just as guilty. I put off life to appease others and I put off life by justifying to myself that I could do it later.

Don't get me wrong. I have loved and experienced so much. But I have also put so much off for later. Guess what? Later doesn't happen. It will always be in the future and unless we can time travel which, as of yet, happens only in the movies, we're stuck in the present.

We are so used to looking externally for self-worth. We look to our achievements, the things we have accomplished, the careers we have had, the home we live in, the possessions we have bought, and the need for perfectionism.

How many of us look at who we are? We are enough as we already are. We are our kindness, our sensitivity, our sense of humour, and the many gifts we have that are unique only to us. Society rarely acknowledges these as valuable, yet they are the very fabric of society. We bring ourselves to our relationships, friendships, and our encounters with others, our own brand of uniqueness. This creates community.

Awareness is the key and self-love is the door that opens it. If we truly learn to love ourselves with all our magnificence, imperfections, and beauty, we will start to value our own worth. I have explored this a lot lately, yet I still trip up. I have recognised my gifts and talents, but I still revert to old habits. It's so easy to do. We have been conditioned to conform, to not stand out, to question our worth.

I was taking part in a creative group that had many successful artists, illustrators, painters, designers, and photographers in it. I entered the meeting hesitantly, thinking I had nothing to offer. I hadn't sold any photographs, hadn't written anything new, or made any money recently from my talents. I was judging myself and my worth on what I had achieved or my perceived lack of achieving.

I suddenly realised what I was doing and stopped. I was part of this group because I was creative, along with everyone else there. I wanted to share my own unique gifts and I didn't need to prove anything. I was enough as I was. It was okay to just be me and that was more than enough. I entered the meeting full of joy and excitement. I was just as worthy as anyone else and deserved to be there.

How many of us suffer from imposter syndrome where we believe that, one day, someone will find out that we are a fraud. That's what I thought when I joined this group but came to realise that I belonged just as much as everyone else. They were also very friendly and welcoming, which helped!

Imposter syndrome is real, yet it's not. It's something we create within our own minds. We feel we aren't good enough, not as successful, not as pretty, not as wealthy, or not as accomplished as others. What if someone finds out that we are only faking it? What if they think we are a fraud?

The term imposter syndrome[39] was coined by two psychologists, Dr Pauline Rose Clance and Dr Suzanne Imes in their 1978 study on high-achieving women who questioned their talents and suitability for certain roles.

It appears to be less common in men because they are often validated and praised for their accomplishments. Women, on the other hand, have worked hard over the centuries to have their careers, independence, and their existence recognised. Very often it is the men they work with who question their authority, and society still relegates them to second-in-command.

No wonder so many women feel they have to prove their worth!

We create stories around our worth and we convince ourselves that they are true. We doubt our innate gifts and talents. We forget that we are worthy, valuable, and loveable as we are. We start to believe in society's lies. We tell ourselves that we are frauds and question how long it is until everyone else finds out. We may then withdraw just in case and end up perpetuating our fears.

We constantly apologise for our perceived mistakes when no apology is needed. We apologise for getting things wrong, for getting things right, for being too much, for just being ourselves. As my friend Natalie Murray, a deep transformation mentor, says, 'You are not an afterthought, a second-class citizen, an inconvenience, or a burden and you are not required to apologise for yourself anymore'.

I know many accomplished, talented, and successful women who still question their worth. They have senior positions, actively create positive change, and make a real difference in the lives of others. Yet they still have doubts. They still question if they are good enough.

Michelle Obama felt that she didn't belong in an elite school when she was accepted at Princeton University[40]. Even while she was in the White House, she asked herself, 'Am I good enough to be the First Lady of the United States'?

Even after writing eleven books and winning many awards, author Maya Angelou still felt that she hadn't earned her achievements. 'Uh oh, they're going to find out now. I've run a game on everybody, and they're going to find me out.'[41]

Isn't it about time that this changed? Never apologise for who you are. You are necessary. You deserve to be here and are worthy of having an amazing life. By recognising your worth, you are a beacon for every other woman to do the same.

> To forgive is to set
> a prisoner free and discover
> that the prisoner was you.
>
> LEWIS B. SMEDES

CHAPTER TWENTY-THREE
Forgiveness

Most of us are brought up to say sorry for when we do something wrong. When we hurt others or make mistakes, we usually apologise. It is the 'done thing.' Good manners. It's what society expects of us. It also means we can move on and forgive others and ourselves.

Forgiveness is a part of growth. It's something we need to do if we are really determined to let go of the past and grow as adults. It's something we need to do if we want to truly love ourselves and move on.

It can, however, be very challenging. As children, we often begrudgingly say sorry because our parents expect us to, even if we don't necessarily mean it.

When we were children, my sisters and I had one tricycle that we shared. One day, I decided that my younger sister had had more than sufficient time on the trike and it was my turn. So, I told her it was 'red lights' and put up a broom as a barrier for her to stop. She was travelling at some speed and consequently fell off. She screamed enough for our mother to come running. I slowly apologised and lent her my favourite doll—not because she was crying but because I feared I would get into even more trouble if I didn't. After all, she should have handed over the trike.

As an adult, it can become even harder to do. If we feel that someone has hurt us and in turn, we have hurt them, how do we apologise when we feel that they deserved it or hurt us first? How do we forgive people and events that have caused us pain and anger?

Forgiveness is necessary to maintain social relationships and to allow us to move on[42]. It helps us deal with those negative emotions we are holding onto. It's necessary to recognise the emotions we are feeling rather than suppressing them, which is harmful to our health. Forgiveness also allow us to forget, so that we can stop reliving the hurtful event and move on with our lives.

I'm not trivialising forgiveness here because if something traumatic has happened to you, it can be near impossible to forgive. However, it's important to remember that you are doing it for yourself, not the offender. You may need help to do this and that's okay. It's often necessary to ask for help as our emotions can be a minefield to navigate.

However, how many of us learn to forgive ourselves? Being compassionate towards ourself means we show kindness and understanding rather than criticism or judgement. It means looking at the little child who took on certain patterns and behaviours to fit in or protect herself, or to find her way in life and learning to forgive her. Without guilt!

I know that being the 'good girl' and the perfectionist was my way of navigating my home environment. Throughout my life, I placed a huge burden on myself to do things the 'right way' whatever that was. I studied harder, worked harder, and beat myself up over mistakes. 'Perhaps I could have done things a different way'. 'Perhaps I should have asked for help'? 'Perhaps I shouldn't have tried to interfere or said such and such'?

The thoughts running through your head can be endless. Many of us place such a huge burden upon ourselves. We berate ourselves for our mistakes and behaviours when they are often the only way we cope or feel safe. We place huge expectations on ourselves to meet the obligations or needs of others. We people please everyone we meet so that we are liked and aren't judged. We put the needs of others before ourselves and then feel resentful and guilty.

Perhaps it's time to move on and forgive ourselves.

This begins with compassion and forgiving yourself for the past. You can't undo what has been said or done, but you can start to love and forgive yourself.

We are very quick to show caring and compassion towards others, but less so in doing this for ourselves.

Why? Because it is far easier to forgive others than forgive yourself.

We may apologise to others out of a sense of guilt or obligation but apologising to ourselves is much harder. To forgive ourselves for past hurts, we need to respect, accept, and love ourselves. We may not be responsible for what happened in the past but we can begin to change how we treat ourselves. This takes work and takes awareness. Self-forgiveness also means taking responsibility for one's self and there comes a time when you have to draw a line in the sand and say, 'I'm ready.'[43]

Self-forgiveness leads to self-love. And it is incredibly empowering.

After the final no, there comes
a yes. And on that yes,
the future world depends.
No was the night.
Yes is this present sun.

WALLACE STEVENS

CHAPTER TWENTY-FOUR
Yes

How many of us say yes to meet the needs of others before our own? It's a familiar role I took on for most of my life. It's amazingly easy to do.

It's easy to say yes to social commitments when everyone else is going or if family and friends expect you to be there.

It's easy to say yes to working longing hours when your boss demands it or you feel obligated by guilt.

It's easy to say yes to the mothers' committee, or the school fete, or to a million-and-one other tasks that are asked of you.

It's easy to say yes out of guilt or obligation or a perceived sense of duty.

It's easy to say yes to the roles that you feel you need to fulfil to be worthy or acceptable.

But what if instead, we said yes to things we genuinely wanted to do and to things we sincerely wanted to experience or bring into our lives.

What if we said yes to the new job or travel or adventure? Or to that dance class, or that art course, or that new romance, or to the million-and-one opportunities out there for us instead of the million-and-one commitments?

What if we said yes to what our hearts asked of us rather than the 'should's. (You know, that word that needs to be eliminated from the English language.)

What if we said yes to vulnerability?

Learning to say yes to our heart's desires takes practice and courage. It means we open ourselves up to be hurt, disappointed, or judged. But it also means we open ourselves up to opportunity and excitement. To the possibility of adventure and the unknown. To realising our dreams. And that is how we make our lives extraordinary. As Garrett Gravesen says, "I hope you find those 10 seconds of insane courage … to start now."[44]

Please don't feel that all the roles you have taken on are wrong or need to be discarded. We take on roles for many reasons and many of these roles continue to bring us pleasure and great joy. They are a part of who we are. A doctor may love his patients and being part of their health journey, a teacher may love the joy of imparting knowledge, an artist may love the creative process, and a sportsperson may love the challenge of a marathon.

I love being a mother. It has been a huge privilege for me and one of my greatest lessons in life. So has nursing and reflexology. However, I have realised that there is more to me and there are many other roles that I want to be part of. I want to be an author of many books, a photographer of great images, and a painter of delicate and exquisite art.

Will I achieve all these things? I have no idea, but I'm going to have fun trying. I'm going to take action, no matter how scary and impossible it feels and see what the outcome will be.

Whatever role you take on in life, enjoy it, accept it if it serves you, and disregard it if it doesn't. Then look at how else you can stretch yourself. What else fuels you? What do you love doing? What are you passionate about? It doesn't have to be some grand thing. It can be as simple as painting a rose or planting that vegetable bed. It can be dancing around the house or joining a choir. Explore all of you! Then allow yourself to feel uncomfortable. Because you inevitably will.

Change brings discomfort and it often brings fear. We are creatures of habit and the unknown can bring up insecurity and anxiety. What it it's a disaster? What if I fail? What if I'm judged or thought irresponsible? What if I lose my friends? What if it's a waste of money?

Change can be scary. It can make us feel physically ill or keep us up at night. I know how many sleepless nights I have had or how ill those butterflies in my stomach have made me feel? Change threatens our security, the status quo. If we make changes, how will our family or friends react? Will we be criticised or judged? What will everyone say?

So often we are worried about others perceived perception of us, but remember we are not living their lives. We are living our own. Our individual, unique, single lifetime.

Unless we take those steps and take on those challenges, our lives stay stagnant. We never get to experience magic. We never get to experience adventure. We never get to experience the incredible.

We stay safe but is safety all we want? I don't mean the safety of our surroundings or an actual threat to our lives, but the safety of staying the same. The safety of procrastination.

I'm a huge procrastinator. I look at something new from every angle. What if I did it this way? What if I left it until next week? Do I really want to do it after all? Is it worth the effort? Time and time again, I have talked myself out of doing something because it felt too big and scary or I was unsure of the outcome. So, I put it off.

Guess what? We can never be sure of the outcome.

We can plan and plan for weeks on end but the future is unknown. The outcome is yet to happen and it's outside our control. We may make mistakes or things may not work out the way we envisaged, but that shouldn't stop us. We try again and that's how we grow and achieve, often beyond our wildest expectations.

Does the risk of failure mean we don't do it? Edmund Hillary took up the challenge and said 'Yes' to climbing Mount Everest. Da Vinci persisted and said 'Yes' to his inventions. Van Gogh kept creating and said 'Yes' to his art. I'm sure these people and many more have questioned their ideas and probably procrastinated doing them, but their desire to create, to make a difference, to step out of their comfort zones and try something new, overcame their fears and doubts.

They weren't guaranteed of success but they went out and did it anyway. They said yes to the challenge. Yes to their dreams.

This doesn't mean that their dreams always worked out or they never revised their vision. They didn't try and control the outcome. Rather they were open to making changes as they needed to. Vincent Van Gogh actually painted seven versions of his famous "Sunflowers", five of which hang in galleries around the world today[45].

They refined their inventions, dreams, and creations until they achieved their goals.

It's the same whenever we start something new. We develop an idea or a dream that we want to bring to fruition. We explore the possibilities and whether they seem feasible.

We need to be realistic but must never discount our vision. We may want to climb Mount Everest but is this likely now? For most of us probably not, but if you really want to do this, explore how you can make it a reality. Then comes the difficult bit. We talk ourselves out of it.

I'm not fit enough, not clever enough, not creative enough. Many of us then move onto something easier. Something that is far removed from our dreams, but easier to attain. We tell ourselves that we didn't really want it anyway.

But what if we want a different life? What if that little voice inside our head keeps chattering? What if it persistently reminds us that yes, Mount Everest, or that painting you want to sell one day, or that song you want to record or that story you want to publish is still possible?

Then by God, listen to it!

Find out how you can reach that dream. Maybe you need to do a course, or just practice your art, or start fitness training and climbing smaller mountains first? Make enquiries. Find out. Ask questions. Olympians all started with a dream.

Many of us may not want to go to the Olympics, but I'm sure every one of us has dreams.

If you want to find out who you really are, start saying yes to yours.

There is a candle in your heart,
ready to be kindled.
There is a void in your soul,
ready to be filled.
You feel it, don't you?

RUMI

CHAPTER TWENTY-FIVE
Open Your Heart

How do you open your heart when you have been hurt before? When life has dealt you heartache and pain, how do you present with an open heart? On your journey to find yourself, it's important to ask this question.

Was I living with an open heart, speaking my truth, and sharing my opinions and thoughts? I certainly hoped so, but, deep down, I knew that there were parts of me that I still kept hidden. After all, I had become an expert at that.

I knew that to live from my true essence, open up to all that the Universe had in store for me, I needed to live with an open heart. Now I know that the term Universe has been bandied about by so many lately. To me, it means Wholeness, Spirit, or God, whatever you believe in. A divine power greater than myself. You may believe in it or not, but for me to find my true essence, the wholeness of who I am, I do believe in something or someone greater than myself. After all, the Universe encompasses all of humanity.

So, I looked at how I was living with an open heart, how I was opening up to the Universe, and what was stopping me. I had found my voice and was speaking up and expressing more of me. But I knew that there were still hidden parts that I kept silent. You know what I mean. Those thoughts or ideas or actions that you think are silly or will be judged. The ones that you think people will laugh at or criticise because they think it's childish, or risky, or too outrageous, or too grand.

And what if they are!

What if our ideas are amazing or outrageous? Why do we fear what others think or say? It's that old voice inside that questions our worth and society's expectations of us. It's the roles we have taken on in life that have kept us safe and secure. It's the roles where we feel comfortable and unchallenged.

Isn't it time we ditched them and said goodbye to other people's views on how we should live our lives? Isn't it time that we stopped living the life others expect us to live? Isn't it time that we lived life on our terms?

After all, we only have one life so why not live it the way we choose to.

I know that it's not always easy to forget the past. If your parents or friends didn't support your decisions or questioned your choices, you probably began to doubt yourself. If your family or peers criticised your career, or your writing, or the way you dressed, you often conformed to their expectations. I know that I did. After all, I wanted to be loved. I wanted to fit in and be accepted. In fact, I wanted to be validated for my very existence. How many of us do that?

Being praised because you followed a certain career path, or stepped up to meet others' expectations of you, means that you belong. When society accepts us, when we belong, and when we fit in with society's expectations of us, we don't face judgement or criticism. We conform and we are smiled upon.

However, if we question authority, our upbringing, or the views of our family and friends, we rock the boat. We challenge the norm and this appears threatening and uncomfortable to others.

Well, let me tell you. We are not here to make others comfortable!

Our life is our own. Yes, we need to live within society's rules and not break the law or else anarchy ensues, but the very essence of who we are depends on us being truthful with ourselves.

Our opinions matter. Our choices matter. The decisions we make matter. Maybe not to everyone else, but they matter to us. To really open your heart means to accept all parts of you. The funny and loveable parts and the not so nice, yucky parts. We all have them. That's part of being human.

To open your heart means that you need to show all of You. To not be afraid of upsetting others because you think differently. To not be afraid to say no when you need to. To not be afraid to share your dreams, even if they seem illogical or impossible.

So, I began to share my writing and my poetry. I began to share my photos. I began to share my opinions even if others disagreed. And guess what, no one died. The world didn't end. In fact, I received support. Others began to share their own dreams and vision. Others accepted my boundaries and didn't question them (well, at least not to me). Those that did, I said goodbye to. I explained my reasons but it was up to them if they accepted them or not. I was staying strong.

This was the new me.

As an author and spiritual leader, Marianne Williamson says, "And as we let our own light shine, we unconsciously give other people permission to do the same."[46]

Yes, some of my photos were rejected, and my writing didn't always express what I wanted to say, but I was opening my heart to possibility. I was painting pictures that might one day hang in a gallery. I was taking photos that might one day grace someone's walls. I was writing stories and poems that might one day sit on someone's bookshelf.

How can you open your heart? By taking that chance, by putting that record out, by writing that book, by creating that jewellery, by changing your job, by sharing more of you. By being open and authentically you. Yes, some might not like this and feel threatened by all the changes in you, but hey, that's okay.

You're only bringing up their own fears and insecurities. You owe it to yourself to live this one magical, crazy, messy life and do it your way. You owe it to yourself to explore all aspects of you. You never know what you are capable of unless you try. You never know what you may achieve unless you take that first crazy, exciting, terrifying leap and step into the unknown.

Now that's opening your heart!

Our deepest fear is not
that we are inadequate.
Our deepest fear is that we are
powerful beyond measure.
It is our light, not our darkness
That most frightens us.
We ask ourselves
Who am I to be brilliant,
gorgeous, talented, fabulous?
Actually, who are you not to be?

MARIANNE WILLIAMSON

CHAPTER TWENTY-SIX
True Essence

How then do you find your true essence, and what exactly is it? I see it as your soul, the very heart of you. The part that makes you unique and unlike anyone else. I used to think that life would take a certain path, but once I realised that everyone's path was meant to be different, I gave up on conforming to another person's view of life. I gave up listening to society's expectations of me. I realised that I wanted to live a life of meaning. Not a life where all I did was give to others and be the good girl, the obedient one, the responsible one.

Have you let go of the many roles you have taken on in life, the ones that no longer serve you? Have you broken the shackles and stepped out from others' expectations? Have you let go of the guilt and obligations to find out who you really are?

Are you ready to do this?

I know that I wanted to live a life on my terms. I wanted to find true freedom, whatever that meant for me. I wanted a life of ease and flow and meaning, where each morning greeted me with excitement, not dread. I wanted to find my true essence.

So where do you start?

I began to do the things that filled me with joy. Meditation every morning and eating healthily with no guilt about that occasional chocolate or glass of champagne. Walks in nature and being present in the moment. Listening to my body and what she needed. Time with friends or time alone. Family and lots of laughter. Travel and adventure. Seeing my clients, but on my terms. Having strong boundaries around my time and availability, including more creativity in my life to feed my soul.

I started to play.

Play is something that is encouraged in childhood but discouraged and trivialised once we are adults. As children, we were told to go out and play when we were sitting around, bored, or when we were under our parent's feet. Play didn't require much planning. It was usually spontaneous. My sisters and I would play hide and seek or ride imaginary horses around the garden. We made use of whatever was at hand. An old broom or long stick with some rope as a harness was all we needed. A few strategically placed chairs or logs would suffice as jumps and we were off, lost in play for hours.

A forest of bamboo growing behind an old shed was our cubby house. We would host afternoon teas on makeshift chairs and tables with remnants of food scavenged from the kitchen. It was a great place to hide when hiding was warranted. Our play was only limited by our imagination and like most other children, our imaginations were boundless.

As adults, we often forget that having fun and playing is a natural part of life. We have a career, find a partner, establish a home, and conform to what is expected of us as an adult. We may have grown up, but have we grown wiser? 'Play is for children', we are told. 'Don't be silly. Act like an adult'. But I believe that play is just as important for adults as it is for children. While children learn socialising and problem-solving while growing their imaginations through play, adults learn too[47]. Adults learn to relax, become creative, reduce stress, form relationships, and have fun[48].

Play teaches us to be present. When you are playing a game, creating a painting, or reading a great book, you are totally engrossed in that activity. You aren't thinking about what happened yesterday, or the board meeting next week, or what you are making for dinner tonight. You are in the present.

As children, we do this all the time but as adults, we forget. We live in the past or the future. We are constantly worrying about something that has happened, something that we cannot change, or something that may or may not happen but is out of our control. The present is the furthest thing from our minds.

So, we worry and stress and procrastinate. We don't immerse ourselves into the life we're actually living. The present.

As children, the present was our very existence, but we've forgotten how to live this way. Perhaps we need to be more childlike to recapture this way of living.

What did you love to do as a child? Was it discouraged or considered a waste of time? Were you told to stop dreaming, to grow up, and that you're too old for these games? As children we are encouraged to play but only when it doesn't get in the way of study or the responsibilities of more important things. When I was a child, play had its place but it was rarely given priority over the more serious things in life. Luckily today, the importance of play is more highly recognised. Why then can't we, as adults, engage in more play?

When did you last feel totally free and unapologetically you? Was it on your last holiday or do you connect with this feeling every day? When did you last laugh out loud or do something that others may consider silly? If not, why?

I think that many of us worry too much about what others may say. We want to be accepted and not criticised so we stay sensible. But does it serve you to be sensible all the time? What would happen if you tried something different that your peers may frown upon? Would you be labelled as strange or different. If so, would it really matter?

Wouldn't it be more important to be authentically you?

When did you last jump in a puddle just to feel that extraordinary splash? Or shuffle though mountains of autumn leaves to hear that crunching sound under your feet? When did you last sit on a swing to fly through the air one more time? When did you last see the world through the eyes of a child?

What if you jumped in the ocean with your clothes on because it was such a glorious, warm summer day? What if you sang at the top of your voice because you loved that song on the radio? What if you painted something bold while sitting in a park with your easel? What if you lay on the ground in public to catch that perfect photograph?

Would the world end? I don't think so. We spend so much time worrying about what others may say or think that we miss out on the fun and the opportunities that present in that unique moment. We miss out on spontaneity. We miss out on play. We stop ourselves from being our authentic, true selves.

How then can we find our true essence? How can we find that inner child that still exists in all of us?

We can start by calling in our muse.

She is always there, just waiting to be heard. She may have been silent for some time, even apparently absent, but she is always there. She often visits me at night as I am drifting off to sleep. Ideas and creations suddenly fill my mind. Words of wisdom fill my soul.

Sometimes I gently ask her to return in the morning, but other times she is more insistent, urging me to get out of bed. I quickly write down the words and thoughts that pour forth onto scraps of paper.

Who is this muse? She exists within all of us. She is that inner voice, that intuition, that guidance that fuels our creativity.

She is the ideas that flow out of us, the art, the photography, the pottery, the paintings, the drawings, the books, the dance, and the play that we create.

Do not ignore her for you are only ignoring your own wisdom. Listen to her and you will create magic.

Find your inner voice, your sense of self, and you will find your true essence.

Make the most of yourself...
for that is all there is of you.

RALPH WALDO EMERSON

CHAPTER TWENTY-SEVEN
Be Yourself

Many of us believe that we need to have a purpose in life while we are on this earth. We may feel that a certain career path will give us this purpose or we conform to society's expectations of us and find it that way.

However, these pathways may not bring satisfaction or fulfilment or it may only be fleeting. As we grow older, we may find that we are still yearning for more.

If we let go of our roles and the personas we have taken on, will we feel lost or empowered? Will we feel adrift or find we are more connected to our life?

Once we find our true essence, will this define our purpose?

Joseph Campbell talks about the Hero's Journey[49] where a hero or heroine has an adventure, faces some sort of crisis or adversity, and is put to the test. He or she initially resists change but then grows and learns through their experience, often with the help of others, and eventually comes through victorious.

Perhaps life is just like that.

As we go through life, we all have different experiences. Many are wonderful but others are sad, challenging, and scary. As we grow, we learn about ourselves and others and, hopefully, become better human beings.

As the years pass, I don't see purpose as some gigantic goal. Nor do I see it as some major achievement that if I don't attain, I risk failure. I used to think that I had to be the most dedicated nurse, the most successful reflexologist, the most talented photographer. Not anymore.

Instead, I see my purpose as small steps that I take throughout my life. Each step takes me forwards, backwards, or sideways, depending on how much I learn from my experiences. These steps, when taken authentically and in alignment with who I am, lead me to a sense of fulfilment and joy. A sense of wonder and discovery. My own heroine's journey.

My purpose may not be some grand scheme of saving the world, but instead, one of enriching the people and world I interact with. The more I continue to grow and love myself and give out love and kindness to others, the more I can inspire others to be the best versions of themselves.

To be true to myself is my purpose.

I believe we are born with the essential essence of who we are. Our sense of humour, kindness, creativity, love of nature, our intelligence, our capacity to love, all dwell within us.

Sometimes this essence is quashed, denied, or buried deep down within us due to our upbringing, negative experiences, or the opinions and expectations of others. Sometimes we are ashamed, embarrassed, or fearful of showing our true selves.

But as we grow, learn, and heal through life, we can reignite that spark. It doesn't take much. It can be that one word of encouragement, one gesture of love or kindness, or the one person who believes in you.

Then suddenly the flame is lit. And there is nothing stopping you!

Finding your true essence means being authentically you. This sounds rather obvious but it takes courage to truly be yourself. I recently read a comment on social media, where someone asked 'How can you be authentically you'? The answer to this seems obvious. Just be yourself! But what does that really mean?

How can we be ourselves when we may have spent a whole lifetime being the person that everyone else expects us to be? How can we know who we really are when we have conformed to others' views and expectations of us?

If I'm quiet, people will think I'm boring. I used to think that when I went out with groups of friends. If I force myself to chatter and make conversation when I really don't feel like it, I will be considered entertaining. If I stay out until the wee hours of the morning when I would rather be in bed, I am considered fun.

How often have we changed who we are or the way we were feeling because it seemed more acceptable?

We often emulate others because we feel we 'should' be more like them. If I'm more outgoing, more organised, more happy, sad, or conforming—add what you like. If I'm more of something or someone else, I will be more successful, more accepted, or more liked.

We can never be more of something. We are who we are and by accepting ourselves as we are, we allow our true light to shine. How do we start doing this? By learning to love ourselves, accepting ourselves, and knowing ourselves. By showing compassion towards ourselves. By knowing our self-worth. By letting go of our fears.

I have a beautiful, vivacious sister. She is intelligent, chatty, and the life of the party. But she is not me.

I have a friend who is up at six every morning to clean and tidy her house. Consequently, her home is always immaculate. She is a very active person and gets a million things done every day. But she is not me.

I have another friend who's a fabulous cook and can create an amazing meal from a few basic ingredients. But she is not me.

Society encourages us to emulate others. Advertising and social media are full of seemingly more beautiful, talented, and accomplished people who we can become if we lose weight, wear certain clothes, or buy a specific type of face cream.

We are told that we are not enough as we are, so we need to buy certain things or look a certain way to be better versions of ourselves. We are repeatedly told that we need to improve ourselves and think that we are not acceptable as we are. Who are we kidding?

In fact, we are already more than enough.

We are all born with gifts and talents. We may not all be on the front page of a best-selling magazine, but these images are usually false. They encourage us to aspire to be that certain person in an effort to sell the magazine. Society encourages this and advertising feeds on it. If we believed that we were already perfect, we wouldn't need to buy all these products. So, we are told that we need improvement. We are told that we are not perfect. That there is room for improvement. That we could be better.

As human beings, we learn as we journey through life. We make mistakes, we fall, we pick ourselves up again and continue on. As we grow, we learn kindness, happiness, how to give back to our communities, and a sense of where we fit into our world. We take on careers that hopefully showcase our talents and then we'll be able to make choices and move on if they no longer serve us. We form relationships with those we love and care about and we have experiences that are both challenging and exciting.

We have our human frailties but they are part of our makeup, of who we are. We may not be the most famous composer, or the winner of a major tennis tournament, or the inventor of a cure for all cancers. Instead, we have our own unique talents, our own unique gifts.

We may have an amazing sense of humour, a warm heart, or always sing in tune. We may paint beautiful paintings or create stunning gardens.

Our diversity is a gift and one which we should encompass. With open arms.

Be authentically you and don't worry what others think.

When we were living in England, there was an upmarket ladies clothing store in a town near my home. It sold some lovely, albeit expensive, clothes, but I had never been inside. My friends claimed they never shopped there as they felt intimidated going in and the staff were all pretentious.

I decided to give it a try. After all, the shop assistants were there to serve me.

Mustering up my courage I entered the store and smiled sweetly at the shop assistants and said a cheery hello. I declined offers of help and spent some time looking at the beautiful clothes.

I didn't try anything on or buy a single item, but I felt proud of myself for not listening to my fears and feelings of inadequacy. I may not have been wealthy or been able to buy their clothes right at that moment, but no one knew. As social psychologist Amy Cuddy once said, "Fake it 'til you make it,"[50] and I was certainly doing that. I continued to visit that store and eventually was able to buy the occasional outfit. And I was welcomed every single time!

Don't let fear stop you. Fear is an important mechanism as it protects us from danger. This is necessary when we are being followed in the dark or facing someone or something that is threatening us. It's part of our 'fight or flight' response and serves us well. However, we also initiate this response when we fear change or someone else's opinion or judgement of us. We become anxious and scared of what might happen, even if it never eventuates. Our hearts race and we prepare to flee.

What if we accepted that certain situations were challenging? That some people would criticise us, no matter what we did? That we might not succeed the first time we tried something? That we might fall and fall again? That we make mistakes? Do we just give up and play small forever? Do we grow old and wish we had done things differently?

I certainly don't want to.

Be comfortable in your own skin. Be comfortable with who you are, your strengths and weaknesses. Recognise what you love to do and what you don't and stay true to yourself. Let go of others' expectations and do what lights up your heart.

I love eating out, but don't like hosting huge dinner parties.

I love seeing my friends, but prefer catching up in small groups.

I love parties and dancing, but I am not the life and soul of the party. I prefer to chat quietly in a corner.

I love going out but not every night. Once a week or even once a month is fine by me.

I love seeing musicals at the theatre, but a few times a year is plenty.

I love travelling and adventure, but I don't like going alone. I do, however, get a thrill when I accomplish something that I'm scared of, like attending a conference interstate on my own.

I love walking, but I would never want to do a marathon.

I love holidays, but I don't like sharing with friends. My time with my family is precious.

I love the company of others, but my own time is even more important to me. I need stillness and quiet.

I can admire these traits in others but don't need to emulate them myself.

Being your true self may seem achievable when life is flowing smoothly, but what happens when a crisis or catastrophe occurs. Amid our fear, anxiety, or grief, we often revert to our old patterns. We become the people pleaser once again. The one everyone can lean on. We say yes to appease others who are also distressed, ignoring our own needs.

Why do we do this? Because in the midst of adversity, it's much easier to revert to old patterns. Deep down we know they no longer serve us, but we also know that old patterns are easier to take on. They are comfortable, even when they don't help us. They are familiar, even when they take away from our own needs.

Change is scary and new behaviours take time and effort to take on board. When we are stressed, it feels much easier to become our old selves.

Perhaps then, this is the biggest lesson of all. To be ourselves, even in the face of adversity. To support ourselves when we most need it. Sure, others may need attention too, but if we don't support our own needs, we can't be there for anyone else.

Being authentic is hard work, but the rewards are worth the effort. Don't beat yourself up if things fall apart or if old behaviours come to the fore. Change doesn't happen overnight. It takes time and it takes awareness so embrace all of you. After all, you are learning to be your authentic self and that can be a huge adventure on its' own. Be gentle with yourself and be patient. Most of all, celebrate each new action that you take.

Be aware of yourself, your needs, and what you love to do. Follow this in life and you will be closer to finding your true essence.

How does you know that you are there? That your true essence has been discovered?

How does it feel?

Have you ever read a book or listened to a song that touched your soul, the very heart of you? And you feel it resonating so deeply that it brings forth tears? Have you felt the pure joy of a sunset or the thrill of riding a wave? Have you stood by the ocean and felt excited about just being alive? Have you felt the deep love between yourself and another? Remember that feeling?

That is your true essence. The very heart of you. The fragile, warm, loving part of you that makes you want to get up every day and live.

As Socrates is quoted as saying, 'Know thyself'.

Know what you like and don't like. Know your own nature and live according to this. Start to recognise what brings you joy, what you want more of in your life. Let go of what no longer serves you or doesn't bring you happiness. Look at the many roles you have taken on in life. Hold on to the ones you still love but gently release those that no longer bring you pleasure.

Find the courage to be this person. Live the life you want on your terms. Yes, this may not always be easy or possible, but be authentically you.

Ultimately the journey is one of self-love and acceptance. That's what I have found. The more I have learnt to let go of other's expectations and the burdens I had placed on myself, the more I discovered who I really was. When you find this and really love and accept yourself as you are, you will discover that within this lies your true essence.

And isn't that the best journey you could possibly take?

The best day of your life is the one on which you decide your life is your own. No apologies or excuses. No one to lean on, rely on or blame. The gift is yours — it is an amazing journey — and you alone are responsible for the quality of it.

BOB MOAWAD

CHAPTER TWENTY-EIGHT
Where To From Here?

You began this journey as a quest for discovery, or I certainly hope you did.

Maybe, like me, you realised that there was more to your life, much more than you had been living.

Maybe, like me, you realised that the beliefs and behaviours that you held on to so tightly no longer felt aligned with your vision.

Maybe, like me, you realised that your life was your own and you got to make the decisions.

How do I keep evolving, you may ask yourself? For there will come a time when you start to question where you are headed and who you are. The answers may be starting to emerge, but you are still unsure of your direction. You're recognising more of your own essence but still feel unsure. What happens now? Where to from here?

What steps do you take now to bring this one glorious, exciting life of your dreams into reality?

First, acknowledge how far you have come.

You have begun to accept yourself for who you are. You are beginning to love and honour yourself and are starting to prioritise You. You are gaining a deeper understanding of who you are and finding joy in your own essence. You are starting to live life on your terms.

Boundaries are being enforced and you are learning to say no when circumstances and events don't suit you. You are beginning to say yes to things that light up your soul. Your courage is growing and the real You is emerging from her cocoon. That little butterfly is beginning to spread her wings.

This is indeed magical, for within our growth lies the secret to living an authentic life. Never underestimate how much you have achieved.

You are a shining light and, though it may not feel like it, you have come SO far.

Remember that no grand plan is needed. Just small steps every day to follow your dreams.

Each day in our life is an opportunity to learn. We grow through our experiences, our jobs, our relationships and our interactions with others. If we are open to healing past beliefs and behaviours, we can open our eyes to endless possibilities, through our own personal growth.

Magic happens every day!

Of course there will be setbacks. There always are when we try to change past behaviours and patterns. But that's okay. Know that you are taking action, no matter how small, and be gentle with yourself. Don't blame yourself when things go wrong. Life is all about learning and we don't stop growing and learning until the day we die.

Keep believing in yourself. You are capable of SO much more than you believe is possible. Keep believing in the impossible. Take action on the things that light you up and fill your soul.

Doubt and anxiety may creep in, but don't let them take hold. You are stepping out of your comfort zone and that feels scary. Don't let it stop you.

I, too, often doubt myself and wonder if I will achieve all of the things that I dream about. Will I ever write a best-selling book and get a publishing contract? Will I ever sell my photos, stories and art and make an income from them? Will I have an impact on others, inspire them and make a real difference in their lives? Will I have the resources to travel the world, or as many places as I want to visit in my lifetime?

I have lots of dreams and ideas that surface all the time. They are exciting and sometimes scary, but they fill me with hope. They may not all come to fruition but I can only try.

Time flies by so quickly. Do not waste a precious minute.

Life is meant to be lived, boldly and unashamedly! Choose this one audacious, outrageous and exciting life.

However, don't be despondent if this isn't the path for you. Not everyone holds the same vision.

I know a few people who stayed in the same jobs and worked for the same companies for the whole of their working lives. They raised a family, had a career, then retired to play golf.

There is nothing wrong with this. Our choices are all different and very complex. Financial security, life's circumstances, a need for stability or control or a fear of change can all influence our decisions.

But there comes a time, especially (I believe) for women, when all that they have done and achieved is not enough. As women reach their fifties and sixties, and perhaps even before then, the obligations of the past no longer hold. Their roles as career women, parents and carers may no longer apply or have the same urgency that they once did.

Their children are growing up, and the careers and jobs they have may no longer hold the same attraction.

Women may begin to question who they are and exactly what life holds for them. Of course, this may happen to men too as they get older. But many men lead lives of great self-belief. Society dictates this. Men rarely question their existence or the need for self-realisation.[51]

As I mentioned previously, the roles of men and women throughout history were and continue to be very different. Yes, women have a lot more freedom now than they ever did, but there is still an inequality in pay and positions of power.

Though women have made huge inroads in these areas, they are still poorly represented in areas of influence. While many women hold important jobs, the majority of CEOs, well-paid corporate positions, prime ministers and presidents are men.[52]

Women therefore often question their worth. Society's expectations of them and the roles that they should take on, their experiences growing up and their encounters in the workplace all influence their confidence and sense of self.

But it doesn't have to be this way. Though society may take years to change, we as individual women can make a difference and influence society through our own actions.

Self-love, self-compassion and a deep sense of self-belief can lead us to question the life we are leading. If we are unhappy with our current lives, we have the ability to bring about change. Examine your life and look at what is working and what isn't.

If this is you, and I certainly hope it is, and you know deep down that another life awaits you, then don't settle for the mediocre. Don't be that person who is comfortable with the ordinary. Choose the less-travelled path, the more exciting, challenging, terrifying and exhilarating one.

Then, start to take action!

Even if we have the best intentions in the world when it comes to changing our situation and our current lives, if we don't take action, nothing happens. Everything remains the same. We may make promises to ourselves, download new meditations and surround ourselves with positive thoughts or affirmations, but, without action, our dreams remain just that: dreams!

We put off these dreams, these promises to ourselves, and the visions we hold of the future, until one day we realise that it's finally our time! A time when the obligations of child-rearing, having a career, and caring for elderly parents begin to change and an opportunity arises to fulfil these dreams.

We all experience this transition. However, we all deal with it in different ways.

We may look forward with excitement, or we might procrastinate. Our ego tells us that certain circumstances need to exist for us to move forwards. So we convince ourselves that we are too busy, and we wear our busyness like a badge of honour. We tell ourselves that we are too tired, and that we have too many obligations and commitments now.

So we hesitate. We postpone our lives. We let fear hold us back: Fear of change. Fear of disrupting the status quo. Fear of upsetting those we love. Fear of trying something unfamiliar and new.

So we continue on as we have always done. We stay in the same unsatisfying jobs, the same unhappy relationships, the same repetitive lives. We may not even be particularly unhappy, yet we fear doing something different. We fear exploring the possibilities. We give up on our dreams. We let the hope inside of us wither and die.

But what if this little voice inside of you continues to speak more loudly?

What if it persists and wakes you in the middle of the night?

What if it follows you throughout the waking day?

What if a restlessness sets in and you are lucky enough to feel it?

Then, by all means, listen! Listen to that voice and allow nothing to stand in your way!

You know that more awaits you. You know that an ordinary life is not for you.

Allow yourself to be restless.

Count yourself lucky that you crave for more.

Allow yourself to answer that voice.

It will only get louder if ignored.

Allow yourself to step up bravely.

You are capable of so much more.

Allow yourself to come first.

You have this one amazing life.

Live it.

Author and inspirational speaker Mary Anne Radmacher said, 'Courage does not always roar. Sometimes courage is that small voice at the end of the day saying, 'I will try again tomorrow.'[53]

Yes, obstacles may present. Yes, you may take a few steps backwards. Yes, you may even fall. But unless you believe in that dream, that little voice that guides you, that inner knowing that life holds more, you will never learn to find your path.

NEVER underestimate how powerful you are!

There is freedom waiting for you,
On the breezes of the sky.
And you ask,
"What if I fall?"
"Oh but my darling,
What if you fly?"

ERIN HANSON

CHAPTER TWENTY-NINE
A Time To Fly

I finally realised that everything I had done in the past had brought me to this day. All my past learnings and mistakes had not been in vain. They all made me the person I am right now. I was beginning to accept and welcome this new season of my life.

I, too, had reached that age when my previous roles no longer held any appeal for me. My son was an adult, had left home and was living overseas again. My husband had retired some years previously and was busy with his own activities. I was still running my reflexology business, but, deep down in my heart, I knew that this phase of my life was also ending. I was growing restless and I knew that this restlessness meant I had to change.

My heart was yearning for so much more.

The little voice inside of me was clamouring for attention. 'It's your time now,' it said. 'You are allowed to put your needs first. You are allowed to start living the life of your dreams. You are allowed to take up space. You are allowed to do things out of love, not out of obligation. You have the freedom to choose.'

There was a huge awareness in this. So much of my life had been lived as the 'good girl', pleasing others, meeting their needs. Suddenly, this no longer applied.

I didn't 'need' to be there for anyone. I was allowed to be myself. It was safe to do so and this felt incredibly liberating.

A certain freedom occurs when you realise that you no longer have to please others or, indeed, care about what they think or say about you. Unless you are very confident within yourself, which I rarely was: I always worried about how others perceived me. I was scared of judgement and I wanted to be liked. Most of us do.

But with age comes a certain wisdom. A certain 'Who gives a damn?' attitude. I don't mean that you become cruel to others or deliberately set out to hurt them, but you do develop a self-belief, a self-love, and a self-assurance that you may never have had before. You become less tolerant of misinformation and falsehoods. You no longer have time for such things.

Scottish actor, writer and presenter Alan Cumming said, 'I live my life on my own terms. I don't want to conform or follow the pack or "act my age" because that means allowing other people's opinions to dictate my existence.'[54]

A freedom is born to try new things and you become excited to do so. You also develop a certain liberty to 'get it wrong' and do it anyway. No more 'shoulds' or 'have to's.' No more acquiescing to others' demands and expectations.

It was time to do Me.

I began to wind down my business and cut back on seeing clients. I set a timeline for when my business would finally close. The first client I told about my decision cried. I cried too. After all, I was letting go of something that had held my love and attention for eighteen years. It was okay to feel sadness. It was a difficult decision and I sometimes wavered over it, but I knew it was the right thing to do. Deep within my heart, I felt a strong and persistent 'Yes.'

And I also felt a great sense of joy. A sense of ease. A sense of letting go. It was time to do what I loved now. The past had taught me so much, but I knew that there were still so many opportunities for me to explore. I wasn't dead yet!

So I began to journal all the things that I wanted to do with my new-found unlimited time. I started to write down how I wanted to feel. I wanted freedom and to create a sense of spaciousness. I wanted to wake up excited every day or, realistically, most days. I wanted to live life on my terms and not according to a calendar.

I was excited and had so many ideas, but knew from experience that I needed to focus on just one. For now, I would continue writing my stories. Writing really fuelled my soul. The other ideas I could get to later. Otherwise, my energy and attention would scatter.

Perhaps you, too, have decided to change careers, or have begun a new hobby or an activity that you had always wanted to do but had never had the space or time for. How do you feel?

It can be daunting at first. It can be incredibly scary. The income may not be the same and your family and friends may criticise you. They may think you are irresponsible or silly and you may feel judged.

Just remember: it is your life you are living, not theirs. Other than when we are raising our children, we are only responsible for our own lives. No matter how much you want to influence or control someone else's life, this is not your task. Neither is it theirs to criticise, or judge, or control you.

Ichiro Kishimi and Fumitake Koga, in their best-selling book, 'The Courage to Be Disliked,' wrote 'Do not live to satisfy the expectations of others.' By wanting to be recognised, we throw away who we really are and live the lives of others. Not our own lives.[55]

There will always be naysayers, the negative ones who want to put you down. The Tall Poppy syndrome still exists. It is a concept adopted by society whereby someone is criticised or resented because they are successful, or have achieved something great.

It is said to have originated in Roman times when a Roman ruler, Tarquinius cut off the heads of the tallest poppies in his garden as a sign to his son to remove all his rivals by whichever means possible. Today, it is not taken so literally, but is still prevalent as a form of denigrating someone who is successful or wealthy.[56]

Although it is present in many societies, albeit under different names,[57] it is particularly associated with Australia, thought to be due to the country's egalitarian society and culture of giving everyone a 'fair go'.[58]

No one likes a 'show-off' or someone who seems to be more successful than they are. It is generally not acceptable to 'stand out from the crowd'. But what if you do become more visible? What if you speak up and people notice? What if you step up and show the world your gifts and talents? What if you do stand out from the crowd? Will it be life-ending? I don't think so.

Yes, others may not like it, or may resent you for your success, but often that comes from their own lack of self-esteem, their jealousy, or their beliefs and upbringing. Remember that you are not responsible for their behaviour.

Just be yourself!

Learn to love ALL the stages of your life, from the young vulnerable child to the uncomfortable teenager to the wise older adult. All have played a part in your growth and learning. Take courage in who you have become.

When you live a life of your choosing, you not only get to follow your dreams, but you act as a beacon for others to do the same.

You don't need to be a guru or celebrity. It is enough to shine your own light.

Remember that you are not doing this for others. You are shining your light so that you can live a rich, exciting, kind, loving and fulfilled life. When you do so, your light will radiate out and touch the world. As you begin to choose freedom, you become an inspiration for those around you and everyone you interact with.

You may think that nobody is interested in what you have to say or what you can create. But out of the billions of people on this planet, if you can help one single person, you will have made a difference.

Bring on those naysayers, I say. Let them have their time but never let them divert you from your own glorious path.

So how do I begin, you may ask? How do I suddenly change my life when I know deep down that it needs changing?

My advice is to begin small. That doesn't mean that your dreams need to be small. It just means that if you start small, they appear more doable and less terrifying. By all means, start big if that's what you desire but, for those of us who fear change, myself included, starting small feels less daunting.

Create space in your life so that you can find some balance. It may start off with an afternoon or morning just for you. This can then extend to a full, glorious day of 'Me' time. Every time you create space, even if it's space for rest, you allow your imagination to roam. You allow the Muse to come in.

You give yourself the time and space to create magic. You allow yourself to say yes to unexpected opportunities that come your way, because you are more open to them. The stress of saying yes to commitments has gone.

By all means, allow yourself to grieve for what is no longer present in your life. Allow yourself to grieve change. It's okay. It's all part of life. It's part of us gaining wisdom. It's part of our healing.

But then, move on. A new and exciting world awaits you.

Know that age does not define you! Nor should it stop you. You are never too old to try something new. Yes, physically, you may not have the body of a twenty-year-old, but there is still so much you can do and achieve in your life.

Motivational speaker and author Louise Hay didn't found Hay House Publishing until she was sixty years old, and she was eighty-one when she released her first film, 'You Can Heal Your Life: The Movie.'[59]

Colonel Harland Sanders was sixty-five when he established the Kentucky Fried Chicken chain.[60]

Julia Childs, author and celebrity chef of French cuisine, was fifty-one years old when she made her TV debut.

And Gladys Burrill began her marathon running career when she was eighty-six and finished a marathon at the age of ninety-two, the oldest woman ever to do so.[61]

Anything is possible if you set your mind to it.

As I started to make these changes in my own life, I realised how much freedom I had been depriving myself of. Yes, I had days off, family time and holidays, but on a day-to-day basis I felt tied to obligations. I had loved my nursing career but it was a career filled with huge responsibilities. I loved my reflexology business and the wonderful clients that I treated, but this too carried responsibilities with it. I knew it was time for something new.

I craved freedom and a life of my choosing. A life where creativity was foremost. A life where the Muse regularly played.

Maybe it comes with age and maybe this varies for all of us, but a certain wisdom begins to grow within you and you know deep down that there are still so many more exciting experiences waiting for you.

You begin to see possibilities that you never could envisage before. You realise that your body needs the care that perhaps you never gave it, while it has patiently been screaming out for attention. You become more aware of your mortality and of everything that you want to do with your life. You realise that, although you feel exactly the same as you did twenty to thirty years ago, your body is not the same. It'a great time to take stock and embrace preventative measures so that your health remains optimal moving forwards.

Healthy eating, taking more exercise - especially of the weight-bearing variety, any necessary scans and your mental health all deserve your attention.

You begin to value your close relationships more and realise just how precious they are and have always been. You begin to make room for what is important and let go of the trivial.

You feel empowered by your actions. You let your purpose fuel you and, even if you don't really know what that purpose is, you follow your heart.

This is not a time to waver. Be curious about everything you do as if it were the first time.

Don't wait for perfection. Embrace being imperfect - it's how we learn. Just take action.

And if you fall, then don't give up. Show compassion towards yourself and try again or try something new. The whole world awaits you and the magic that only you possess.

Holding on tightly to something familiar only holds you back from something new and even better. Step out of the shadows. A whole exciting, brilliant light is waiting to shine upon you. You never know how high you can fly.

Never underestimate your uniqueness and the radiance emanating from you. The world needs you and all you have to offer. Know that, by sharing your gifts and talents, you are enriching the lives of others.

No tall poppies here. Just a cheering choir of other women who are going through the same feelings, worries and fears and who share your trepidation and excitement in all that you are creating in your lifetime.

Be proud. Be very proud.

You are powerfully honouring yourself and are just as full of wonder as the deepest oceans and the brightest star in the night sky. See the beauty around you and recognise the beauty that you also hold within your heart.

By expressing the truth of who you are, you are empowering others to do the same.

You are a beacon of hope and inspiration and I celebrate your journey in this world.

Acknowledgements

It is with a deep sense of gratitude that I would like to acknowledge the people in my life who have made this book possible. To Neil and James, thank you for your love, support, and belief in me and for always being there for me. You have never doubted my passion and have always been there to listen and offer suggestions.

To my sister, Cathy, for her encouragement and love and for supporting all my writing endeavours. Your advice and unwavering belief in me are greatly appreciated. Thank you for sharing your childhood memories with me and reminiscing on the past.

To the wonderful Leesa Ellis and her Team at 3 ferns, namely Judith and Keith. Thank you for your advice, support, patience, and understanding. I truly appreciate being part of your publishing world. I could not have written this book without you.

Lastly to all the family and friends that have shown interest and confidence in my ability to write and complete this book. You have all inspired me. Thank you.

References

Chapter One

1. King, Margaret L. "Women of the Renaissance." The University of Chicago Press, 1991.
2. Lota Brown, Meg and Boyd McBride, Kari. "Women's Roles in the Renaissance." Greenwood Publishing Group, 1995.
3. Hurl-Eamon, Jennine. "Women's Roles in Eighteenth-Century Europe." Greenwood Publishing Group, 2010.
4. Wayne, Tiffany K. "Women's Roles in Nineteenth-Century America." Greenwood Publishing Group, 2007.
5. "Women in the 19th Century: Introduction"; Feminism in Literature: A Gale Critical Companion. Encyclopedia.com https://www.encyclopedia.com/social-sciences/encyclopedias-almanacs-transcripts-and-maps/women-19th-century-introduction.
6. Simkin, John. "Marriage in the 19th Century." Spartacus Educational. 1997. https://spartacus-educational.com/Wmarriage.htm.
7. "Women's Roles in Nineteenth-century America."
8. "Equal Pay for Women." National Museum of Australia. December 16, 2022. https://www.nma.gov.au/defining-moments/resources/equal-pay-for-women.

Chapter Two

9. Abrams, Rebecca. "Minding the Baby." The Guardian, July 16, 2004.
   https://www.theguardian.com/books/2004/jul/17/highereducation.booksonhealth.

10. Gerhardt, Sue and Matthes, Michiel. "Why Love Matters: How Affection Shapes a Baby's Brain," *Improving the Quality of Childhood in Europe*, 2 (2011): 80-97.
    https://www.researchgate.net/publication/343583160_Why_Love_Matters_How_Affection_Shapes_a_Baby%27s_Brain.

11. "Man of the House." Thesaurus.com, Roget's 21st Century Thesaurus Third Edition, 2013.
    https://www.thesaurus.com/browse/man%20of%20the%20house.

12. Burkett, E. "women's rights movement," *Encyclopedia Britannica*, December 2, 2022.
    https://www.britannica.com/event/womens-movement.

Chapter Three

13. Mence, Victoria, Gangell, Simone, and Tebb, Ryan. "A History of the Department of Immigration: Managing Migration to Australia." Commonwealth of Australia, 2017.
    https://www.homeaffairs.gov.au/news-subsite/files/immigration-history.pdf.

Chapter Seven

14. Howes, Carollee. "Friendship in Early Childhood." In *Handbook of Peer Interactions, Relationships and Groups,* edited by Kenneth H. Rubin, William M. Bukowski, and Brett Laursen, 180–194. Guildford Press, 2009.

15. O'Connor, Pat. "Friendships Between Women: A Critical Review." *Guilford Series on Personal Relationships* (2023).
    https://www.researchgate.net/publication/232530025_Friendships_between_women_A_critical_review_Guilford_series_on_personal_relationships.

16. Eldemire, April. "Why Friendships are Vital to the Health of Your Relationship." Psychology Today, May 30, 2019. https://www.psychologytoday.com/us/blog/couples-thrive/201905/why-friendships-are-vital-the-health-your-relationship.

Chapter Eight

17. Nania, Rachel. "Why Prioritizing Motherhood in First 3 Years is Critical." WTOP News, May 19, 2017. https://wtop.com/parenting/2017/05/why-prioritizing-motherhood-in-the-first-three-years-is-critical.

18. "Fathers Impact Child Development." *Focus on the Family Australia.* 2009. https://www.families.org.au/article/fathers-impact-child-development.

Chapter Nine

19. Arthur, Art and Tors, Ivan, creators. *Daktari.* Directed by Paul Landres, featuring Marshall Thompson, Cheryl Miller, and Hari Rhodes. Aired 1966–1969, in broadcast syndication. MGM Television.

20. Reuters. "6 Tourists Who Were Seized in Zimbabwe Said to be Dead." *New York Times,* June 13, 1983. https://www.nytimes.com/1983/06/13/world/6-tourists-who-were-seized-in-zimbabwe-said-to-be-dead.html.

Chapter Ten

21. Marshall, Helen. "Childless by Choice by Jean E. Veevers. 220 Pp. Butterworths, Toronto 1980. Price $16." *Children Australia* 6, no. 3 (1981): 22–23. doi:10.1017/S0312897000012959.

22. Chrastil, Rachel. "How to be Childless: A History and Philosophy of Life Without Children." Oxford University Press, 2020.

Chapter Eleven

23. Croce, Jim. "Time in a Bottle." Recorded 1972. On *You Don't Mess around with Jim*. ABC Records, vinyl LP.

24. Springsteen, Bruce. "Thunder Road." Recorded 1975. On *Born to Run*. Colombia-Sony, vinyl LP.

Chapter Twelve

25. Conservators of Ashdown Forest, https://ashdownforest.org.

Chapter Thirteen

26. Dorfner, Micah. "How You Can Enjoy the Empty Nest." Mayo Clinic News Network. Mayo Clinic, September 27, 2017. https://www.mayoclinic.org/healthy-lifestyle/adult-health/in-depth/empty-nest-syndrome/art-20047165.

Chapter Fifteen

27. Hay, Louise L. "You Can Heal Your Life." Eden Grove Editions UK, 1988.

Chapter Sixteen

28. Australian Institute of Health and Welfare. "Informal Carers." Commonwealth of Australia, 2021. https://www.aihw.gov.au/reports/australias-welfare/informal-carers.

Chapter Seventeen

29. Mate, Gabor. "When the Body Says No – The Cost of Hidden Stress." Scribe Publications Australia, 2019.

30. Roosevelt, Franklin D. "Franklin D. Roosevelt Inaugural Address." March 4, 1933. Transcribed by The American Presidency Project. https://www.presidency.ucsb.edu/documents/inaugural-address-8.

31. Lipton, Bruce H, Ph.D. "The Biology of Belief." Hay House UK, 2005.

32. Soghomonian, Ida. "Boundaries – Why are They Important? Part 1." The Resilience Centre, September 23, 2019. https://www.theresiliencecentre.com.au/boundaries-why-are-they-important.

Chapter Eighteen

33. Gravesen, Garrett. "10 Seconds of Insane Courage." Baxter Press, 2017.

34. Ibid.

Chapter Nineteen

35. Pert, Candace B, Ph.D. "Molecules of Emotion." Simon & Schuster, 1999.

36. Matthews, Dona, Ph.D. "Children's Problem Behavior Understood through Brain Science." *Psychology Today,* February 8, 2019. https://www.psychologytoday.com/us/blog/going-beyond-intelligence/201902/children-s-problem-behavior-understood-through-brain-science.

Chapter Twenty-One

37. Bassi, Nicola, MD, Amital, Daniela, MD, Amital, Howard, MD, Doria, Andrea, MD and Shoenfeld, Yehuda, MD. "Chronic Fatigue Syndrome: Characteristics and Possible Causes for its Pathogenesis." IMAJ 10 (2008): 79–82. https://pubmed.ncbi.nlm.nih.gov/18300582.

38. "The Biology of Belief."

Chapter Twenty-Two

39. Tushyand, Ruchika and Burey, Jodi-Ann. "Stop Telling Women They Have Imposter Syndrome."; Harvard Business Review, 2021. https://hbr.org/2021/02/stop-telling-women-they-have-imposter-syndrome.

40. Obama, Michelle. "Michelle Obama Describes Her Battles with Imposter Syndrome." The *Guardian*. December 4, 2018.

41. Cox, Elizabeth. "What is Imposter Syndrome and How Can You Combat It?" TED Talks.

Chapter Twenty-Three

42. Noreen, Saima, Bierman, Raynette N. and MacLeod, Malcolm D. "Forgiving You Is Hard, but Forgetting Seems Easy: Can Forgiveness Facilitate Forgetting?" *Psychological Science* 25, no. 7 (2014): 1295–1302. doi:10.1177/0956797614531602.

43. Woodyatt, Lydia, Wenzel, Michael and de Vel-Palumbo, Melissa. "Working Through Psychological Needs Following Transgressions to Arrive at Self-Forgiveness." *Handbook of the Psychology of Self-Forgiveness* (2017): 43–58. doi:10.1007/978-3-319-60573-9_4.

Chapter Twenty-Four

44. "10 Seconds of Insane Courage."

45. "5 Things You Need to Know About Van Gogh's Sunflowers." Van Gogh Museum Amsterdam. https://www.vangoghmuseum.nl/en/art-and-stories/stories/5-things-you-need-to-know-about-van-goghs-sunflowers.

Chapter Twenty-Five

46. Williamson, Marianne. "A Return to Love: Reflections on the Principles of A Course in Miracles." HarperCollins, 1992.

Chapter Twenty-Six

47. "Why Play Is Important." *Raising Children AU.*
https://raisingchildren.net.au/newborns/play-learning/play-ideas/why-play-is-important.

48. Robinson, Lawrence, Smith, Melinda, and Segal, Jeanne. "The Benefits of Play for Adults." December 5, 2022.
https://www.helpguide.org/articles/mental-health/benefits-of-play-for-adults.htm.

Chapter Twenty-Seven

49. "Monomyth: The Hero's Journey." *Berkeley University of California.*
https://orias.berkeley.edu/resources-teachers/monomyth-heros-journey-project.

50. Hanna, Julia. "Power Posing: Fake It Until You Make It." Working Knowledge: Business Research for Business Leaders. Harvard Business School, September 20, 2010.
https://hbswk.hbs.edu/item/power-posing-fake-it-until-you-make-it.

Chapter Twenty-Eight

51. Kay, Katty and Shipman, Claire. 'The Confidence Gap.' The Atlantic Magazine, May 2014 issue.
https://www.theatlantic.com/magazine/archive/2014/05/the-confidence-gap/359815/

52. The World's Women. Chapter 5. Page 115. 2015.
https://unstats.un.org/unsd/gender/downloads/WorldsWomen2015_chapter5_t.pdf

53. Radmacher, Mary Anne quote.
https://www.goodreads.com/author/quotes/149829.Mary_Anne_Radmacher

54. https://www.instagram.com/alancummingreally/p/DFUIRXROqSB/?hl=en&img_index=1

55. Kishimi, Ichiro and Koga, Fumitake. 'The Courage to be Disliked', Allen & Unwin, 2017. Pages 114, 116.

56. Marques, Matthew D. Tall Poppy Syndrome, Heroism and Villainy. Encyclopaedia of Heroism studies. Living Reference work entry. Pages 1–5. 11 August 2023.
https://link.springer.com/referenceworkentry/10.1007/978-3-031-17125-3_441-1

57. https://en.wikipedia.org/wiki/Tall_poppy_syndrome

58. Duarte, Fernanda with Davel, Eduardo, Jean-Pierre Dupuis and Jean-François Chanlat. Culture and Management in Australia: 'G'day, mate' Chapter VII.5 Pages 18–26, 28–29. 2008

    https://adm3012-plongees.teluq.ca/teluqDownload.php?file=2016/09/chapVII_5.pdf

59. Louise Hay's Legacy. Hay House Publishing. 2017.
https://www.hayhouse.com/louise-hay-legacy#:~:text=In 1987, what began as,, Johannesburg, and New Delhi.

60. Friendship Living. 10 Stories of Successful Seniors. June 25, 2021.
https://www.friendship.us/insights/successful-seniors#:~:text=1.,became a beloved television series.

61. Careline 365. Success over 50. Top 10 Career Success Stories. 27 November 2024.
https://careline.co.uk/blogs/tips/success-over-50-top-10-career-success-stories?

To receive your complimentary Book Bonuses, please visit

judynewbery.com/
book-bonuses

www.ingramcontent.com/pod-product-compliance
Lightning Source LLC
Chambersburg PA
CBHW062033290426
44109CB00026B/2613